Just for Fun

NATURE STORIES IN SIGN LANGUAGE

Just

for

Fun

100,000 students used these supplementary self-teaching ideas -- a thought-provoking resource by Barb Robbins (Robbinspring Publications)

- Activities
- Experiences
- French, Spanish
- Kids Contributed
- Lesson Planning
- Music
- Wildlife Art
- 820 Illustrations

Publisher's Cataloging-in-Publication Data:

Robbins, Barbara H., 1935-
   Just for Fun: Nature Stories in Sign Language
   by Barbara H. Robbins
     p. cm.
   Includes Index and 820 illustrations
   ISBN 0-9630060-0-2 (pbk.)
   1. Sign language. 2. Children's stories (with wildlife art)
   I. Title
   HV2474.R63   1992
   362.4-dc20   91-61687

Manufactured in the United States of America
by Malloy Lithographing Inc., Ann Arbor, MI

Printing paid in part by Consumers Power Foundation, Jackson Society for Handicapped Children and Adults, and The Plymouth-Canton Civitan Club

Cover painting by Catherine McClung. The professional artists retain the copyrights for their work, carefully reproduced with permission. **Do not even think of copying their artwork.**

Wordsign sketches by Jason Graves (with Ivan Graham, Christi Mansfield, and Owen Swinford).

Teaching posters are available (with or without stand-up binders).

A nonprofit educational corporation [501(c)3 - MICS 12521], Robbinspring Publications promotes Sign Language for communication and is staffed entirely by volunteers. Ask your tax advisor about possible deductions for a donation and/or a portion of your purchase price.

Additional copies of this book may be ordered through bookstores or by sending $12.95 (in Michigan, please add 4% sales tax) plus $2.50 for postage and handling to:

     Publishers Distribution Service
     5893 Sullivan Road
     Grawn, Michigan 49637

     For VISA/Master Card orders,
     call: 1-800-345-0096

DEDICATION

This collection honors my lively parents, Ethel and Ray Huntwork, who care. They began taking American Sign Language classes after age 70 – because **my** hearing capability continues to diminish.

FOREWORD

I was so excited when I saw this book for the first time that I wished I was a kid again! Growing up hearing impaired, I could look at the pictures in a storybook, but I could not understand the words. Sometimes even the pictures didn't make sense. I did not know how words were spelled, so the printed letters did not make sense either.

This is a great book because hearing–impaired children will be able to read stories and increase their understanding. It's a fun method of learning two languages – Sign Language and English.

It opens up a whole new world for hearing–impaired children to begin to increase their vocabulary through Sign Language, which provides a better picture of what is being read.

The book, *Just for Fun: Nature Stories in Sign Language*, covers a wide range of topics and activities which each child can use to broaden their knowledge in many areas. It will support each child's participation in their home and surrounding environments and that means they won't feel left out. They will be able to recognize and know there are different species and names of birds, for example.

Barbara has done a fantastic job with this book. It is inspiring and it will motivate hearing–impaired persons, and everyone who reads it, to want to learn more!

Lenore Spagnuolo Coscarelli, M.A., Program Manager
Michigan Association of Deaf/Hearing/Speech Services
and Instructor, Lansing Community College

ANIMAL ACTION

MANUAL ALPHABET

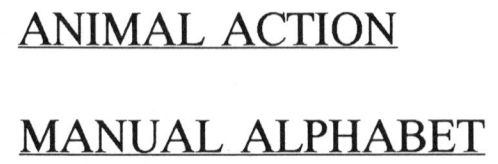

Handsigns by Jason Graves, animals by Michael Glenn Monroe

A

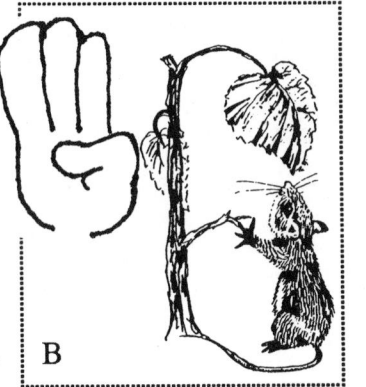

B

C

D

E

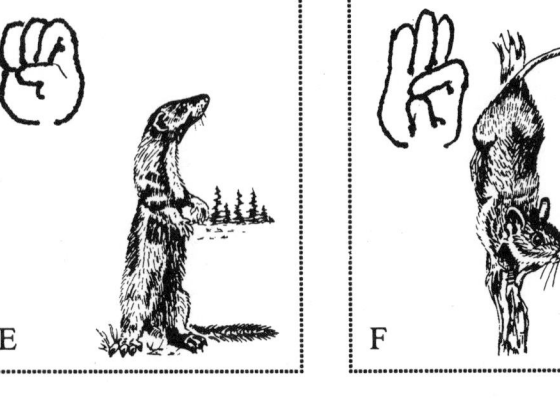

F

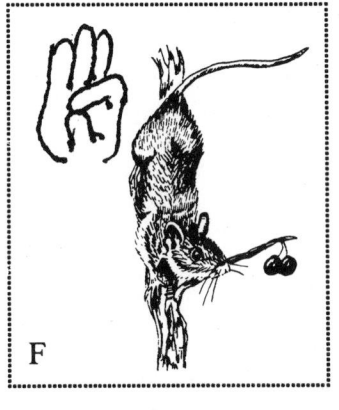

G

H

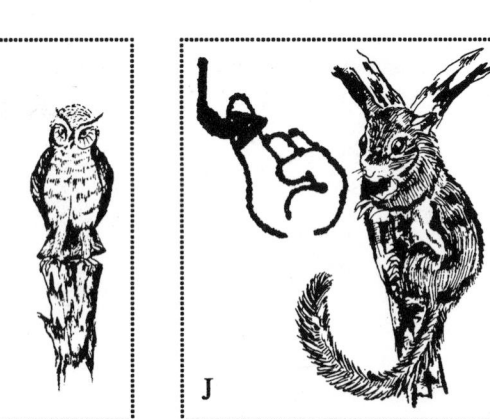

I

J

K

L

M

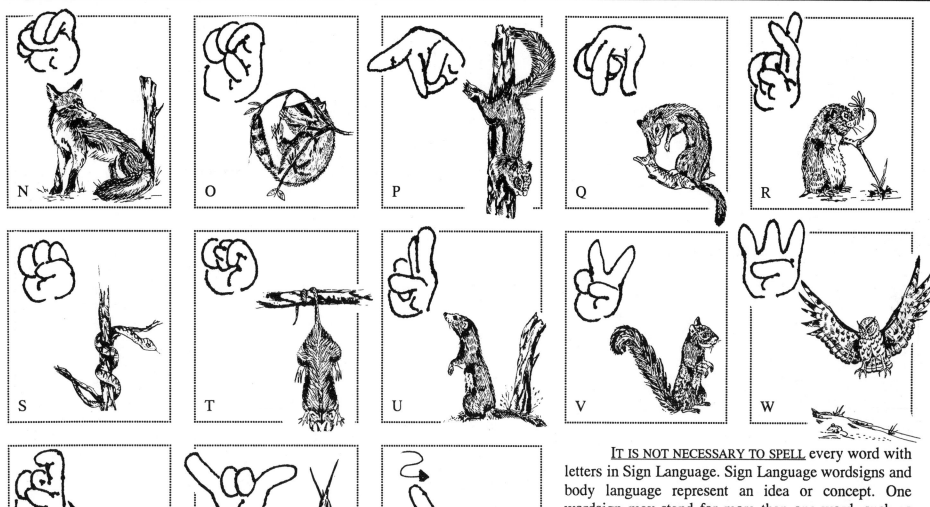

N O P Q R

S T U V W

X Y Z

IT IS NOT NECESSARY TO SPELL every word with letters in Sign Language. Sign Language wordsigns and body language represent an idea or concept. One wordsign may stand for more than one word, such as *pretty* and *beautiful*, or *garden, grow, plant*, and *spring*. However, you will want to use the alphabet to spell names or ideas for which you do not know a wordsign.

"DOTTED" HANDS are used often in our wordsign sketches. The "dotted" hand is the one that you move to perform the Sign.

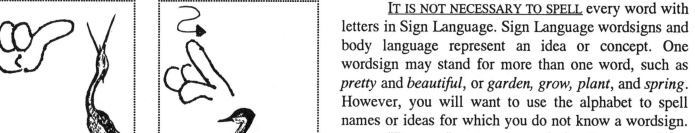

CONTENTS

Sketch by Cindy Lyons

YOU are so smart, you used a sign language before you could talk.

INTRODUCTION

● "I ALWAYS wanted to learn sign language, but...."

● THINK what wordsigns you use every day – "Hi," "Shhh," "Come here," and hugs. How do you show someone how big a fish you caught?

● RESEARCH proved that babies who see Sign Language can use it. At a younger age they can tell you what they want (better than babies who do not know wordsigns) whether or not they can hear.

● ENJOY this way to talk silently with your friends who can hear – at naptime, in libraries, if your throat is sore, or if you are hiking and don't want to scare animals before you get a photo.

● LEARN "word families." All words about men or boys start by pretending to touch your hat or the beak of a baseball cap.

● VISIT an art gallery to see the artwork we reproduced by permission, or Robbinspring will contact an artist for you.

● STORIES about the pictures help us remember the wordsigns.

● YOU WILL WANT to create other stories with the wordsigns.

● I WAS SO SCARED, it took me 15 years to get brave enough to learn Sign Lansugage after doctors told me to. Isn't that silly?

● KIDS in France, Spain, Germany, China, and Japan all learn English as a second language. You understand them, even if they have an accent.

● DIFFERENT areas have different wordsign accents. Your signing (or French/Spanish) does not have to be perfect. Your accent is understood. TRY IT.

● WE RECOMMEND that you invite a local Signer to review the wordsign sketches with you.

How to Talk in the Woods AND STILL SEE ANIMALS

Who

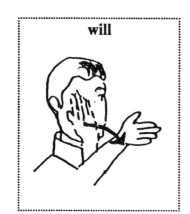

will

jump?

Painting by Tammy Laye

The horse

is outside.

Birds

ride
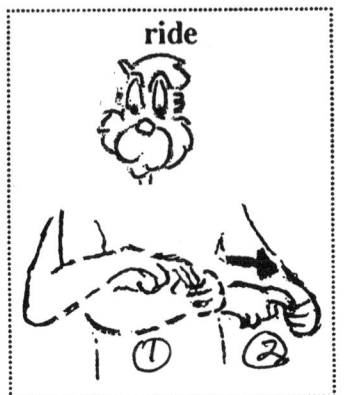

the horse.

Funny!

Painting by Catherine McClung

"I was visiting a friend when I noticed a very old rocking horse out in her yard under the bushes. It had not been used for a long time. I wanted to paint a picture of the antique, so my friend let me take it home for a while. I was surprised to find nuts and tiny seeds in the cracks of the old wood. How do you think they got there? I agree, and that's why I put birds in the painting."

--Catherine McClung

How

to talk

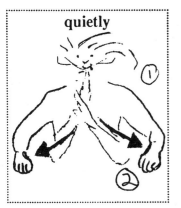

quietly

when it happens--

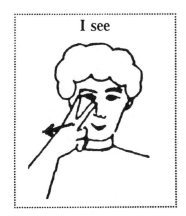

I see

a deer!

Photograph by Carl Sams II

Every morning before dawn, for five years, Carl Sams visited a family of wild deer (even in the winter). Maybe he and his partner talked sign language so they would not scare the deer. See the story and more photos of their adventure in *Audubon* (May, 1987).

Raccoon, 	**what are you doing?**
Looking for 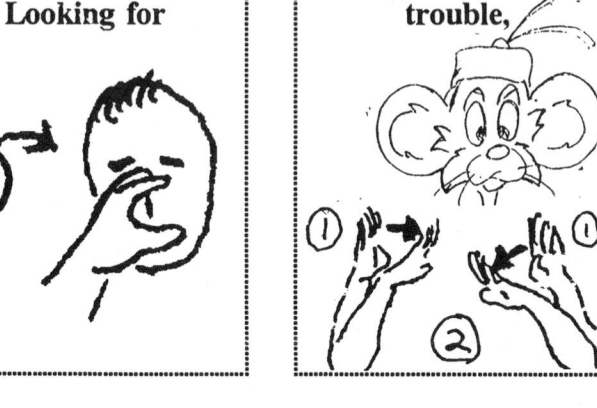	**trouble,**
right? 	**?** 

Painting by Gijsbert van Frankenhuysen

NEIGHBORHOOD TREASURE HUNT – Write mysterious clues on notepaper and pass them out to your neighbors: "Aunt Matilda says your birdfeeder's empty. Please check IN it." "Uncle Herman asked if you got his message with a rare stamp on it. Please check your mailbox." (Think up more, and be sure they have to walk outdoors to solve the mystery.)

The messages they find in the birdfeeder, mailbox, etc. can be like: "Aunt Matilda said you make delicious salads. Please bring one to the Brown's neighborhood picnic next Saturday afternoon." "Uncle Herman challenges you to a horseshoe pitching contest at the Brown's neighborhood picnic."

Any good ideas to be active and have fun outdoors. Right?

How many

men,

women,

dogs

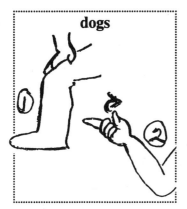

go to

the North Pole?

Painting by Marian Anderson

This painting commemorates Will Steger's expedition in 1986. Photographs and stories are in *National Geographic* (Sept 1986), *Ms.* magazine (Jan 1987), and *Reader's Digest* (May 1988) magazine condensation of Mr. Steger's book "North to the Pole." Ms. Anderson also created a commemorative painting for his team's South Pole trip (*Reader's Digest*, March 1991). See also *Icewalk* 1990 coverage of Robert Swan's international expedition and United Nations award.

FRENCH: Combien d'hommes et de femmes et de chiens vont au Pôle nord?
SPANISH: ¿Cuántos hombres, mujeres y perros van al Polo del norte?

the cat

to go away, leave

the nest.

hears

a bell,

scares

Father

bird;

he

CAT'S CELL

Sketch by Andy Prinz

Animals

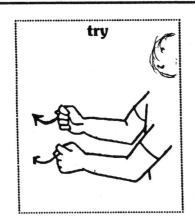

try

to catch

wild

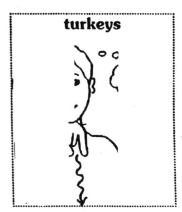

turkeys

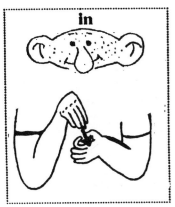

in

the spring.

Keep

Sketch by Andy Prinz

dogs

home.

How
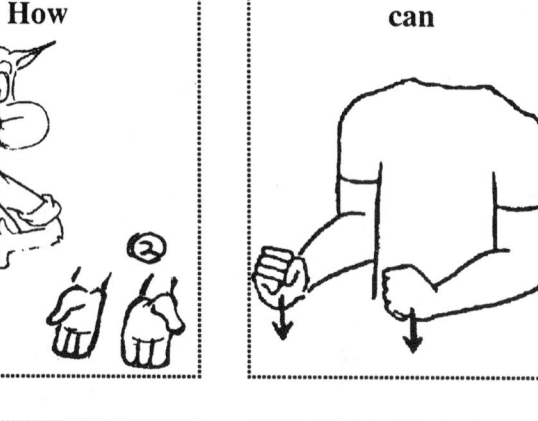

can

we
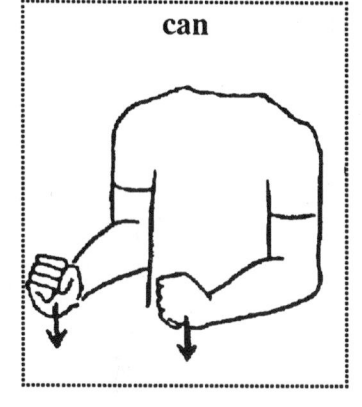

keep

water

clean

where

fish

swim?

Painting by Tammy Laye

FRENCH: Comment pouvons-nous tenir propre l'eau où nagent les poissons?

SPANISH: ¿Cómo podemos mantener limpia el agua en donde nadan los peces?

Grandfather

helps

me

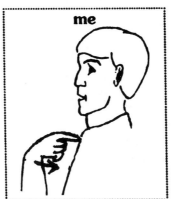

build

houses.

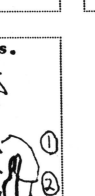

Blue bird

houses.

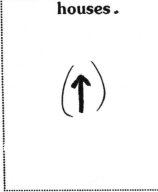

Fun!

Sketch by Andy Prinz

We got a bluebird house at the Bluebird Festival and put it on a pole in our yard, away from bushes and garage.

A pair of bluebirds visited us. They seemed to be house shopping. One bird sat on the roof while the other went inside. Then they both sat on the roof and "talked things over." They flew away for a few hours, returned, and checked us out again. They did not nest here, but came back after a couple of months. Maybe they had a nest nearby and will come to our house next spring. We hope so! They eat the kinds of bugs we don't want.

A bluebird house is not hard to make. You could do it.

Sunday

school

is finished.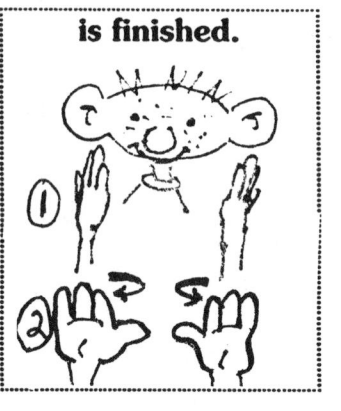

I find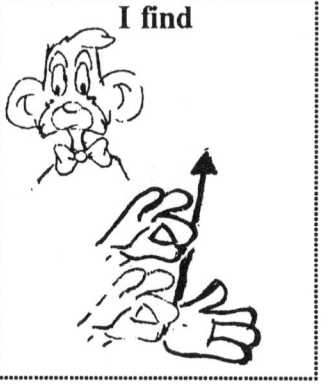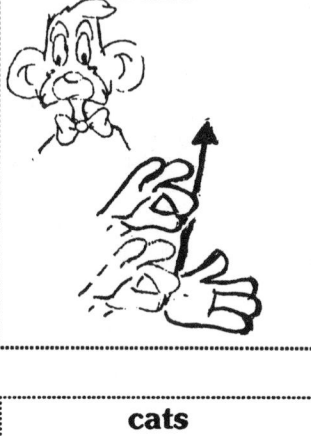

new

baby

cats

(Remember this from page 6?)

in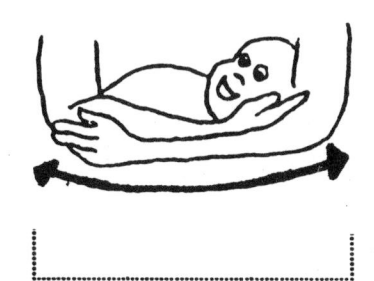

the barn.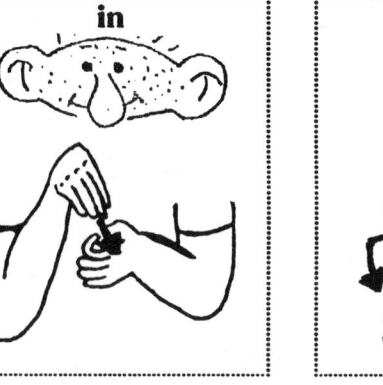

Painting by Marian Anderson

If you can visit or work on a farm, you are lucky. Farms are busy places, but the farm families we know serve communities many ways.

A glorious book, *Country, USA* shows hundreds of photographs taken the same day across the nation. It includes one of the farm at Maybury State Park (Northville, MI) maintained the old-fashioned way, with horses. Some of the photos also appear in *Country* and *Reminisce* magazines. Hike, bike, and photograph for lots of fun.

Little

dogs

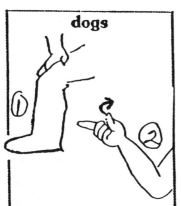

run

climb,

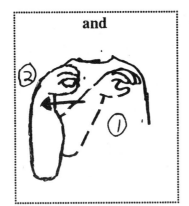

and

tickle

us.

Applause!

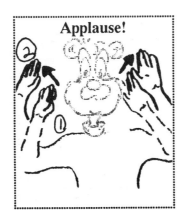

Mike Robbins & Spunky (photograph by Gayle Swinford)

CHARADES PARADE

How many animal names do you know so far? How many action verbs do you know so far? (Teacher, too?)

Rule: NO VOICES ALLOWED!
  You may "yell" the sign for "Applause."

1. Parade in two circles, one inside the other. Girls form one of the circles and boys the other. Choose someone to give a signal for you to stop moving.
2. Girls choose an animal name to sign while marching.
3. Boys choose an action verb to sign while marching.
4. Walk in opposite directions, signing your word.
5. When you see the signal, stop and compare your wordsign with the one opposite you in the other circle.
6. Do they make a good sentence, like "Dogs jump"? Is "fish climb" a good match? Did you laugh at others?
7. Switch – girls sign verbs and boys sign animal names.

NOTES:

Sign Your Own Name:

I am a Visiting Grandmother to school and youth groups. Kids ask me questions like those below. They deserve answers from a voice of experience; but no pity party, please.

"Were you born deaf?"

When I first got the label "hearing-impaired," our children began telling "sneakrets" behind my back. They were about 10, 8, and 4 years old. We grinned at that normal "kid stuff" reaction.

"Is it fun being deaf?"

Is it fun wearing glasses? Is it fun being tall? Is it fun being left-handed? Is it fun riding a bike? Is it fun swimming? Is it fun going fishing? Is it fun baking cookies? Is a birthday party fun? Is it fun reading books? Is it fun climbing trees? Deaf people do all these things. We live life the fun way, the same way you do.

"Deaf" just means eyes work better than ears. Is it fun to "talk" and "hear" through windows? Being deaf is not bad. Being deaf is not sick. Being deaf is "no headaches from noise."

But I don't like making listening mistakes, such as giving "weird" answers because I misunderstood someone's question.

"Can you drive?"

Yes, I drive. I do not hear sirens as soon as you do, but I see the flashing lights. I do not hear trains as soon as you do, but I feel their rumbling. I do not "talk" sign or read lips to help me listen to someone else talk, because I must pay close attention to driving.

(See also page 91 "How can I help?" and page 97 "Will I get deaf?")

Grow With Me

2

A tiny bill has poked a hole in the egg. The chick just hatched the day before (photograph by Gary R. Bortolotti).

Eagle photographs are from the Smithsonian Nature Book, *THE BALD EAGLE: Haunts and Habits of a Wilderness Monarch* by Jon Gerrard and Gary Bortolotti (1988). 1) Jon Gerrard is a medical researcher specializing in blood diseases. His avocation is the study and observation of bald eagles. 2) Gary Bortolotti is assistant professor of biology at the University of Saskatchewan and respected by the raptor fraternity.

Grow	with	me.
	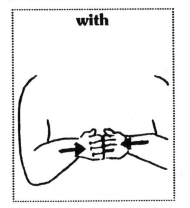	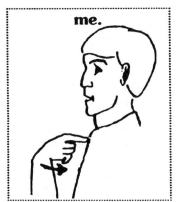

Instructor Note

Most deaf children have parents who can hear and talk. How do the children learn?

Most deaf parents have children who can hear and talk. How do the children learn?

Think about it.

Do the children splash in the tub? Do they paint bright pictures? Do they taste mud pies? Do they love a puppy or teddybear or kitten? Do they watch birds and rabbits in their yard? Do they get sunburned sometimes? I'm not ignoring the questions; they are serious. But we all learn by family experiences. Hugs from Mom and Dad don't have to be heard. Deaf people do learn and teach a little differently than you.

SOME FUNNY THINGS THAT HAPPENED
ON THE WAY TO BECOMING DEAF

Many deaf people, like me, can hear. Understanding the sounds is the trouble. I must have been lip-reading all my life. I had no major problems learning, I guess because I always sat in the front row. Nobody told me to do that. Nobody (not even me) knew I had weak hearing. Thinking back about it, I guess we just automatically adapt.

I remember wondering in 3rd grade, "How did the teacher hear that kid answer from the back of the room?" My sister and I shared a bedroom and played spelling games before going to sleep. I noticed when I began having trouble hearing in the dark. About age 12, I could no longer understand the kids' programs on radio (pre-TV era). But still nobody suspected -- not even my orchestra leaders (I played first chair in the second violin section for seven years).

A nestling Bald Eagle, just three days old (photograph by Gary R. Bortolotti).

NO ONE LIKES TO FEEL "DIFFERENT"

This chapter inspires discussion. The young eagle grows to look as weird as a lonely child feels, yet dares to try new tricks. Allow time for children to express thoughts about this.

The two songs (from birthday party to a mature "...all the powers of the universe are there") are fun to learn. The first is easy because you already know the words. The other is easy because you want to learn..."magic, if you dare." You can teach the school choir to perform it.

Happy

birthday

to you.

Happy

birthday,

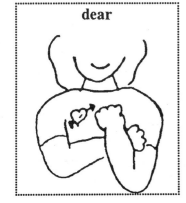

dear

Eagle.

PARTY: Sing and sign your favorite song, "Happy Birthday."

CAKE: For the birthday party, you can make your own good-for-you cake, cookies, and pudding popsicles. We like the delicious MODERN MAGIC MEALS™ brand of foods from our neighbor who is our Amway Products Distributor.

GAMES: Tell a story **without** using your hands! Does this game make you laugh? Is this tricky or hard to do? Maybe you are used to talking with your hands already.

Tape a wordsign on a frisbee and toss it across the yard to a friend. Can your friend "say" the word in Sign Language? Can you "read" the Sign Language word?

An eight-day-old eagle squats in the nest. It is covered with its first of two coats of down (photograph by Gary R. Bortolotti).

Baby

(Remember this from page 10?)

birds

are the same as

children.

All of them

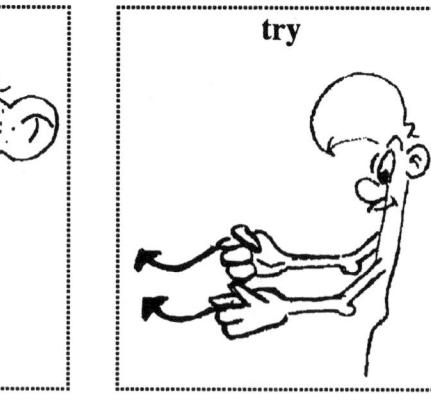

try

An eaglet jumps and flaps in the nest in preparation for its first flight (photograph by Gary R. Bortolotti).

ideas

to learn

how much

we

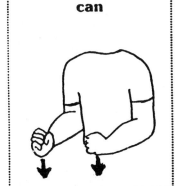
can

do.

Facing into the wind, a young Bald Eagle holds out its long, wide wings to catch the breeze (photograph by Gary R. Bortolotti).

I wonder what happens the first time a young eagle flies and tries to land back on its nest. Do you think it is easy to stop? Do you think they need to try again, with a little different idea how to do it? What if there is not much breeze? I wonder if it is hard for eagles to flap their heavy wings? Is it easier to sail on the wind?

The next story tells what 11-year-old Sarah Deane did when she saw a problem at her school and wanted to help out.

I

have

a friend.

None of

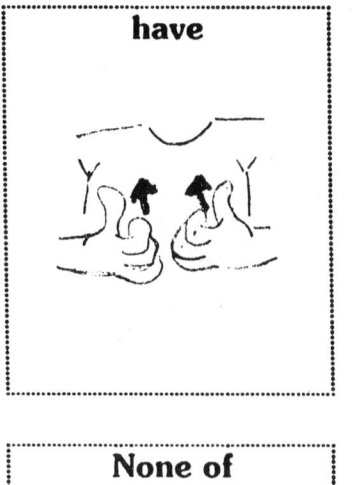

A 20-day-old eaglet. The first down remains in any quantity only on the top of the head. The bulge on the throat is the bird's crop, about one-half to two-thirds full here (photograph by Gary R. Bortolotti).

the kids

play

with

her.

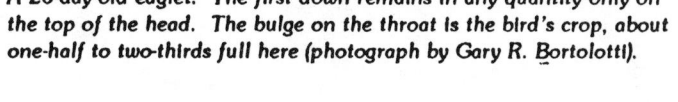

I love you.

I	said,
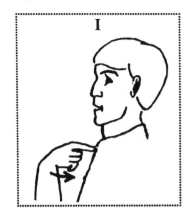	

Sometimes I feel kids leave me alone or don't like me. When I feel that way, I DO something -- ride my bike, or paint our clubhouse, or climb a tree and scream.

"Please	teach	me
	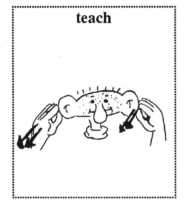	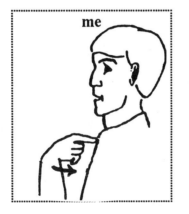

how	to talk with	you."
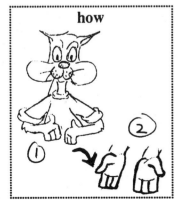		

A territorial adult calls excitedly to an intruder (photograph by Gary R. Bortolotti).

Now

we

play

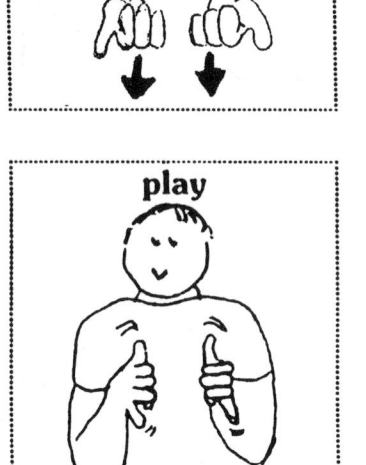

and

Three half-year-old (first winter, known age) Bald Eagles at a wintering site in Maine (photograph by Mark A. McCollough).

eat

together

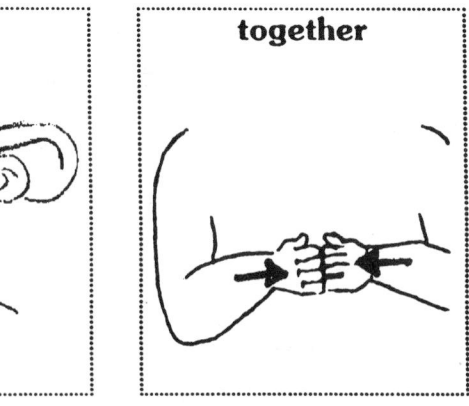

in

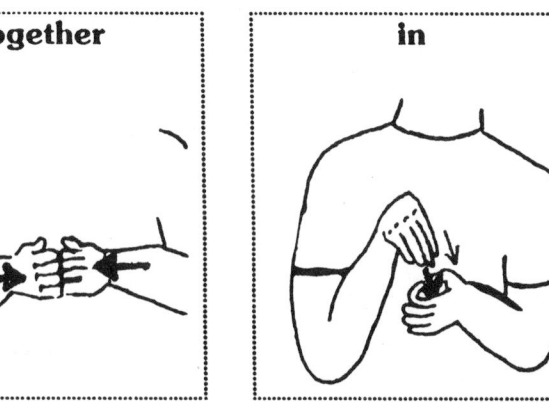

school.

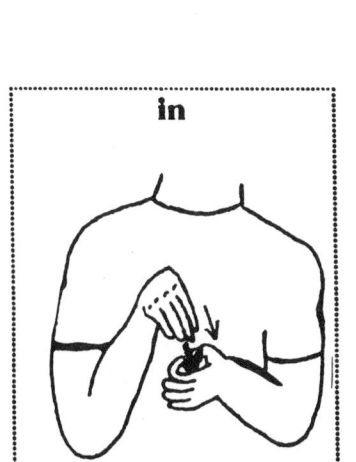

God loves animals and people, if they hear Him or not.

Our

friend,

she

can't

hear.

We

talk

sign

language.

I hate getting teased about:

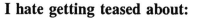

- the braces on my teeth
- my freckles or my scar
- I'm too tall or too short
- misbehaving
- my red hair
- having trouble with math
- missing the ball
- Mom made me dress up, but other kids wore jeans and sneakers

The next five pages are a song written by Marilyn Clayton. Marilyn and her parents studied the French culture and language while living in France. Marilyn teaches French in elementary school in the USA, shares music, and maintains an organic farm with her husband and son.

Request a *FREE* cassette of Marilyn singing her "Live a Life of Magic" song of confidence, when you order another copy of this book. Here's how to sing along with Marilyn--

You

can

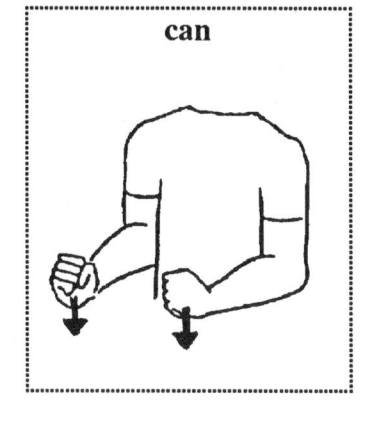

live

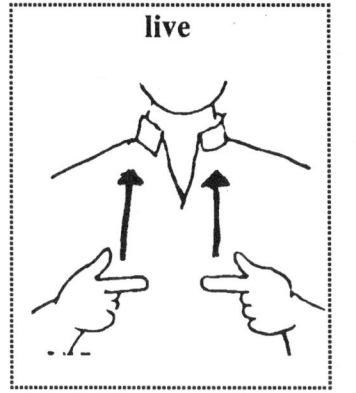

Painting by Jerry Yarnell

a life

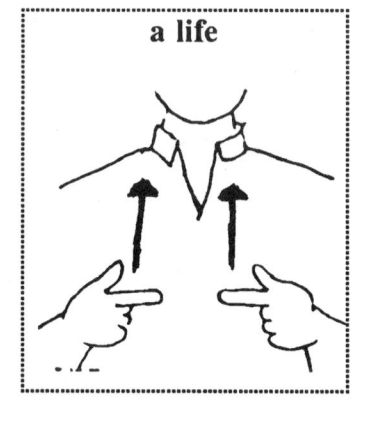

of

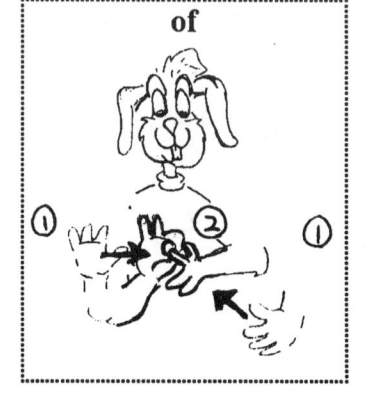

magic

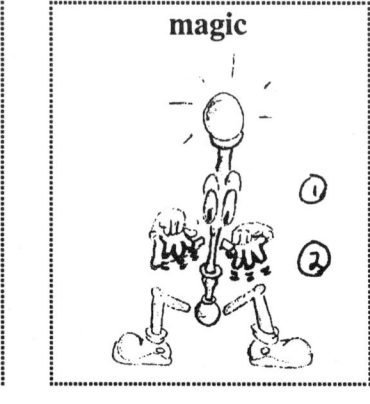

LIVE A LIFE OF MAGIC
--words and music by Marilyn Clayton

if

you

want to.

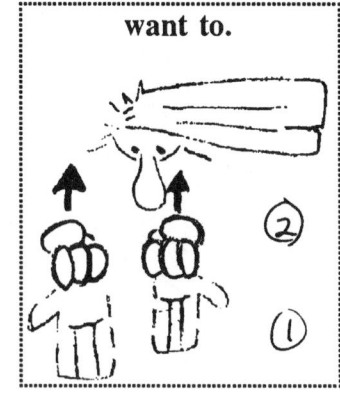

VERSE 1:

1. You can live a life of magic if you want to.

You

can

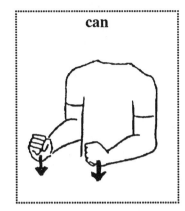

live

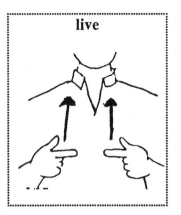

a life

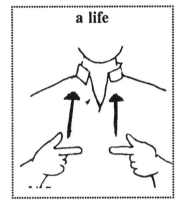

of

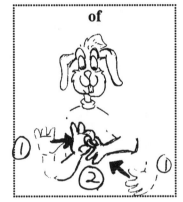

magic

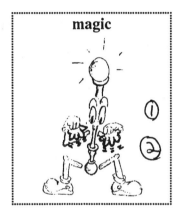

if

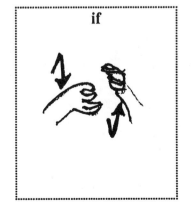

you

dare.

Painting by Catherine McClung

You can live a life of magic if you dare.

to **CHORUS**--

23

All ①

you
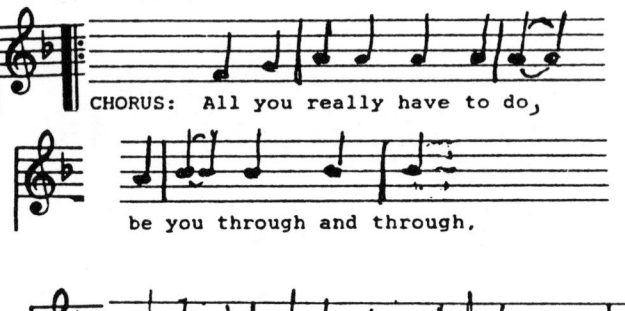

really have to ① ②

do--
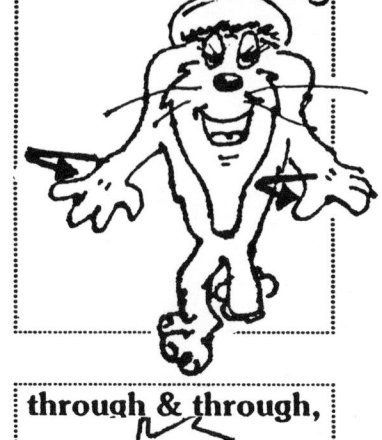

be yourself

through & through,

CHORUS:

CHORUS: All you really have to do,

be you through and through,

And all the powers of the universe are there!

VERSE 2:
You can forgive* your* family* if you want to.
You can forgive your family if you dare.
All you really have to do--be you through and through,
And all the powers of the universe are there.

VERSE 3:
You can overcome* the past* if you want to.
You can overcome the past if you dare.
All you really have to do--be you through and through,
And all the powers of the universe are there.

VERSE 4:
You can laugh* when* you're happy if you want to.
You can laugh when you're happy if you dare.
All you really have to do--be you through and through,
And all the powers of the universe are there.

---

* These wordsigns are on shown Page 26, with Verse 5.

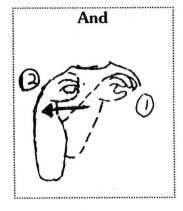

And

all

the powers

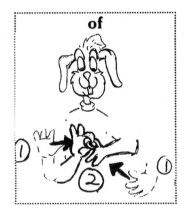

of

the universe

are there.

An adult Bald Eagle about to land (photograph by John E. Swedberg).
--This was one of the top ten national Outdoor Writer photographs in 1989.

Forgive

your

family...

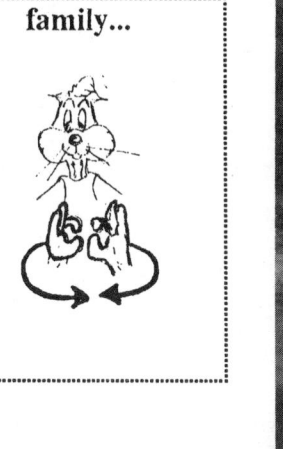

Photograph by Carl Sams II

Overcome

the past...

VERSE 5:
You can love yourself if you want to.
You can love yourself if you dare.
All you really have to do, be you through and through,
And all the powers of the universe are there.

Laugh

when...

<u>CRECE CONMIGO</u> (Traducida al español por Kathryn Mary Stahl, M.A.)

Feliz cumpleaños a ud, querido aguila.

Los pajaritos son lo mismo que los niños.

Nosotros todos tratamos las ideas nuevas a saber lo que podemos hacer.

Yo tengo una amiga.

Ningunos niños no jugaban con ella.

Yo le dije a ella "enséñame a hablarte."

Ahora todos nosotros jugamos y comemos juntos en la escuela.

Nuestra amiga no puede oirnos.

Nosotros hablamos la lengua de señas.

Dios ama a los animales y a la gente si lo oyen a él o no.

<u>La vida mágica</u>.
Ud. puede vivir la vida mágica si quiere.
Puede vivirla si lo atreve.
Todo lo que necesita hacer
es ser sí mismo por completo
y tendrá todo el poder del universo.

        Unas señas mas:
Ud. puede perdonar a la familia si quiere.
Puede perdonarla si lo atreve....

Ud. puede amarse a sí mismo si quiere.
Puede hacerlo si lo atreve....

Ud. puede reirse de sí mismo se quiere.
Puede reirse de sí mismo si lo atreve....

(Spanish translation of this "Grow With Me" chapter)

Follow the ABCs and connect the dots.

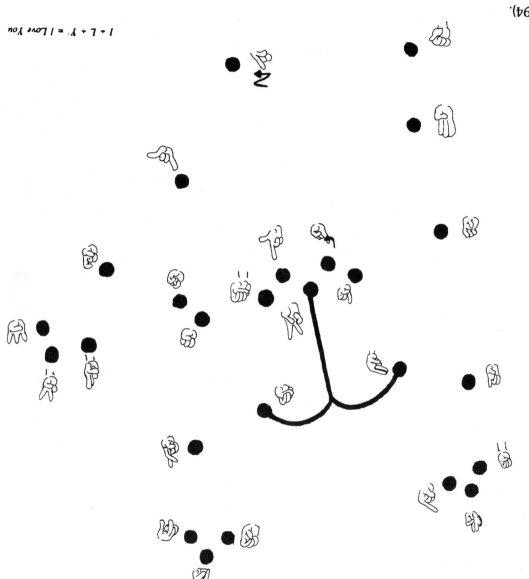

The International "I love you" sign (see Pages 18, 28, 58, and 94).

I + L + Y = I Love You

FINGER SPELLING

Not EVERY word has a wordsign. Words that
don't have a wordsign, like a person's name,
can be spelled using the alphabet shown here.

A	B	C	D	E	F
G	H	I	J	K	
L	M	N	O	P	
Q	R	S	T	U	
V	W	X	Y	Z	

Walk With Me

Etching by Tim Callahan

FRENCH: Marche avec moi.

French translation in this chapter is by Magaly, a 5th grade Back-to-Back exchange student from France.

Walk

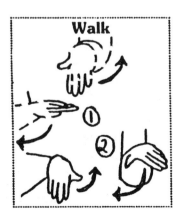

with

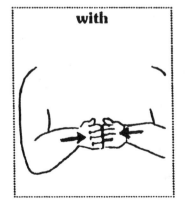

me.

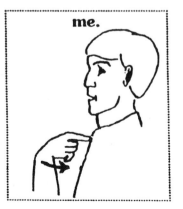

Suggestion for this Section:

Discuss jobs that involve sign language, whether or not the worker can hear:

Operators of heavy construction equipment, like cranes and bulldozers, use hand signals.

Police, diver, coach/referee/teammate and the people in the bleachers, music director, ...

What do pilots and the groundcrew signal when you watch from the airport window?

(See also Chapter 6 "School Daze––Special Skills")

Linda H. was the first salesperson to ask me "Will you please teach me how to Sign? The Deaf people seem to choose me when they come into our store. I guess it's because I'm willing to take time with them. At least, I need to know how to say 'May I help you?'"

Mr. and Mrs. Kohls own both *The Legal News* and *Fax Plus* businesses. For the summer of 1992 they were asked if they would train a Deaf girl on their wordprocessing equipment. They decided to try it. Mr. Kohls said "We did a lot of note-writing to communicate, but she did a good job. Now she is in college."

Don Basye, Treasurer of OUTDOORS FOREVER, provided this chart of signs used by operators of heavy construction equipment when noise prevents conversation (courtesy of International Union of Operating Engineers Local 324, Livonia MI).

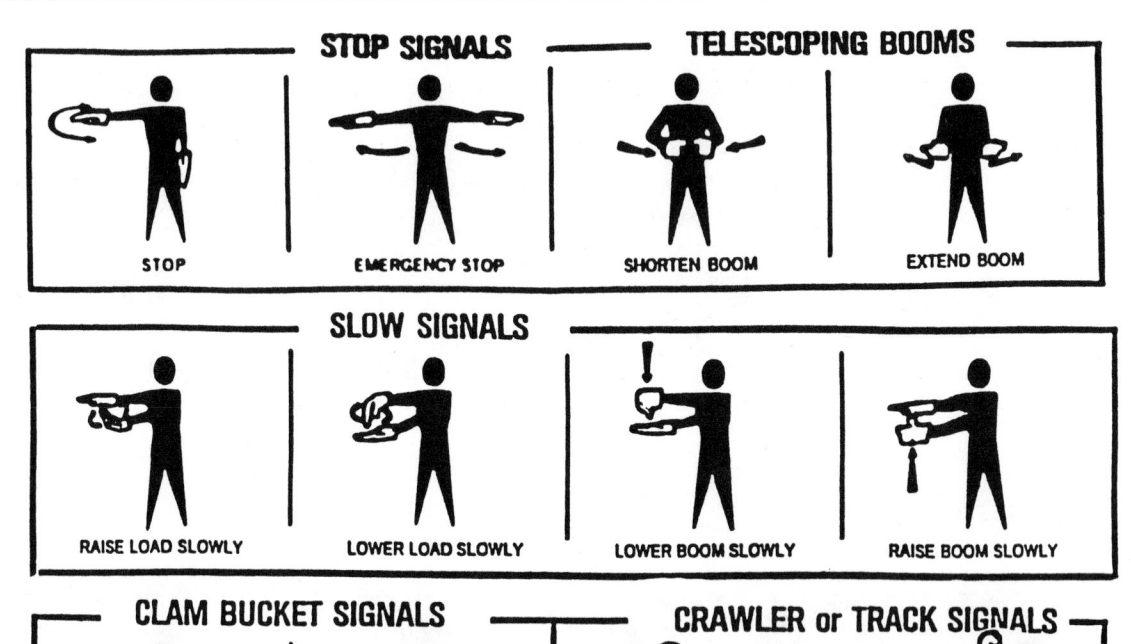

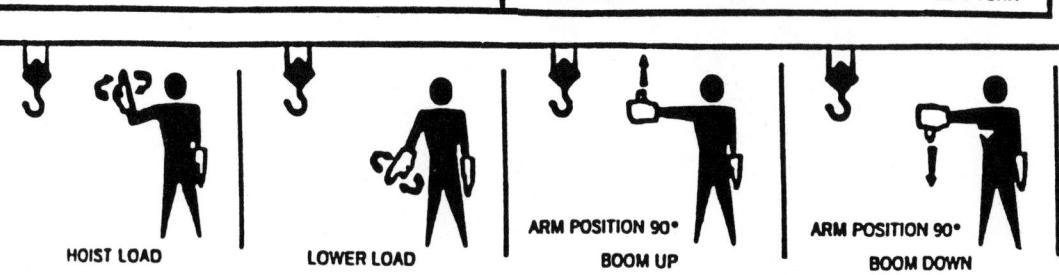

INSTRUCTIONS TO SIGNAL MEN
1. Only one person to be signalman.
2. Make sure the Operator can see you and acknowledges the signal given.
3. Signalman must watch the load – the Operator is watching you.

Wait!

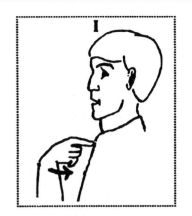

I

want

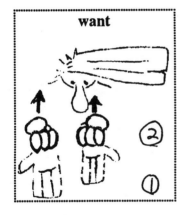

to count

young

geese.

FRENCH:

Attends moi!

Je voudrais compter

les enfants de l'oie.

Painting by Catherine McClung

<u>CATCH THE ANIMALS -</u>
a game requested by Angela
1.   Learn wordsigns in this and other books.
2.   Make flashcards (with the words only).
3.   Choose teams for opposite sides of room.
4.   ANIMALS team uses cards of animal names.
5.   ACTION team uses cards with verbs.
6.   First player signs word shown on first card and runs to get to end of
      other team. Did everyone understand what you signed?
VARIATIONS: Use wheelchairs; sit on and handpush skateboards.

Toads

jump.

What

will

the dog

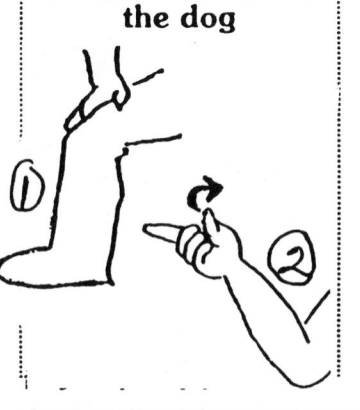

think?

Painting by Tammy Laye

ACTIVITY:

Ask your library for sign language information.
Think of another story to fit this picture.
Write a play to perform in sign language for another class.
Make more wordsign games.
Collect your new wordsign ideas in a sturdy binder.

Listen!

Kids

arrive

home

from

school.

Paintings by Lane Kendrick

FRENCH: Ecoute! Les enfants arrivent à la maison de l'école.

*I really enjoyed your books. My daughter **loves** them!! She is signing left and right. She has also taught herself to sign "The Girl Scout Promise" and "Pledge of Allegiance."*

Thanks a lot!

Tanya Dayton

Three

birds.

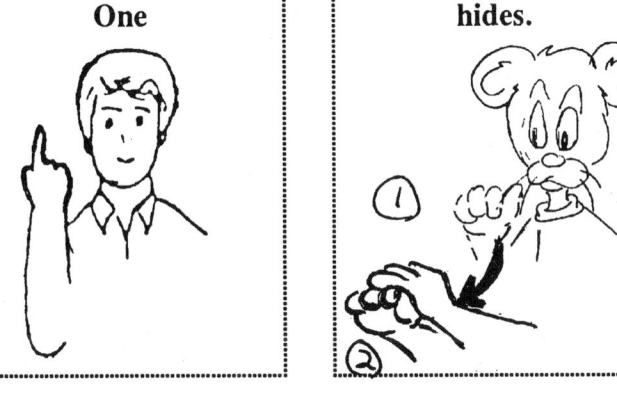

One

hides.

Painting by Bruce Miller

FRENCH: Trois oiseaus. Un se cache dans l'herbe.

ACTIVITY

Request from Owen, for a maze game of some kind, using wordsigns.

Can you think of one that can be easy to explain? We can put it in our next book.

Friends

go for

morning

run.

By 1991, only four states **required** sign language to be available in the schools: California, Maine, Michigan, and Washington.

When did the Americans With Disabilities Act become law? Why were these new rules made?

How and where do people learn sign language?

Painting by Al Agnew

FRENCH: Les amis vont ce matin courir.

SNOWSHOE - a relay to play even without snow. The Snowshoe Relay is played as any other relay with one important difference--the players slide their feet on 8½- by 11-inch sheets of paper. The floor must be smooth enough to permit this. The players move in a manner similar to cross-country skiing or snowshoeing. The relay may be done in any fashion. That is, out to a point and return, or out to the other side of the floor where a teammate is standing. This is a good relay even for a group that is not in particularly good shape.

This game is reprinted with permission from *Aerobics With Fun* by Dr. Charles and Beth Kuntzleman and Michael and Gail McGlynn, Arbor Press, Spring Arbor, MI (1984). It is part of the "Feelin' Good" program.

Cats	**climb**	**and**

I	**like**	**to climb.**
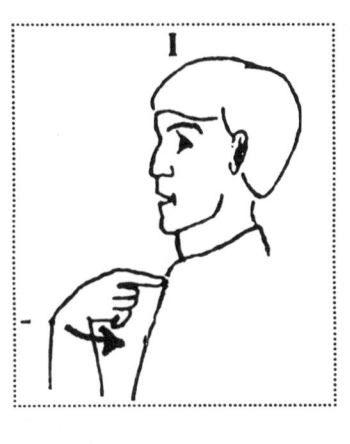	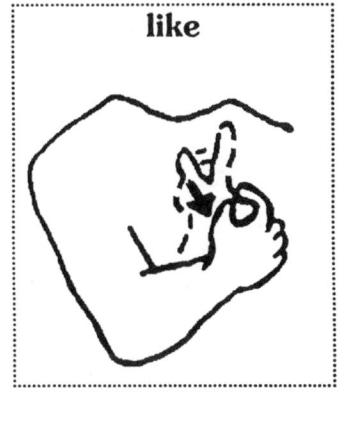	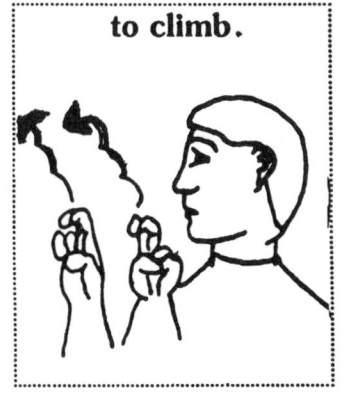

Photograph by Carl Sams II

ACTIVITY

What other animals climb? Can you sign their names? (See Page 90.)

Can you say their names in any other language? (French is on Page 48.)

Painting by Tammy Laye

Raccoons, too.

Painting by Al Agnew

Zero,

one,

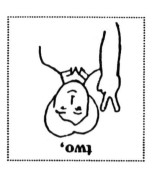

two,

three,

four,

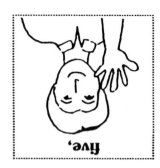

five,

Painting by Catherine McClung

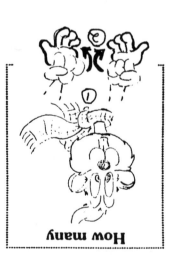

How many

birds

sit

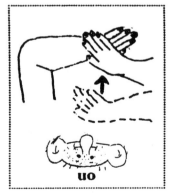

on

a wire?

six,	seven,	eight,	nine,	ten.

Painting by Tammy Laye

When and where does conservation education begin? Where should it begin? Does it start with emotions that swell the childish breast at the first conscious sight of a butterfly, a robin, a dandelion, a field of daisies, a lonely pasque-flower, or mud oozing up between bare toes?

--Ernie Swift in *Conservation Saga*, reprinted from *Badge in the Wilderness* by David H. Swendsen

Painting by Tommy Laye

every day.

things

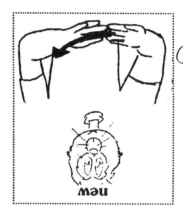

new

learn

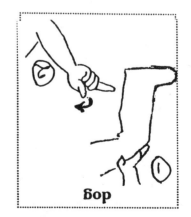

dog

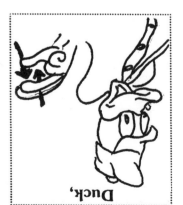

Duck,

Snow!	Play	"Fox	and	Geese."
			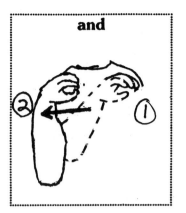	

SNOW ACTIVITY:

1. Stomp trails in the snow. First, a large one almost as big as your yard, then stomp some trails from the outside in to the middle of the yard, like spokes in a bicycle wheel.

2. Choose someone to be "IT," the first "FOX."

3. All other players start in center "nest area" as "GEESE."

4. Fox hollers "SUPPER TIME," and starts ON trail to catch geese.

5. GEESE run ON trails away from fox.

6. Geese who are tagged also become foxes.

7. YOU MUST STAY ON TRAILS.

VARIATIONS:

In school gym or on grass, mark trails with long ropes.

Geese can squat down and waddle.

Fox can run on three legs (like one leg is sore).

Painting by Marian Anderson

Our

family

feeds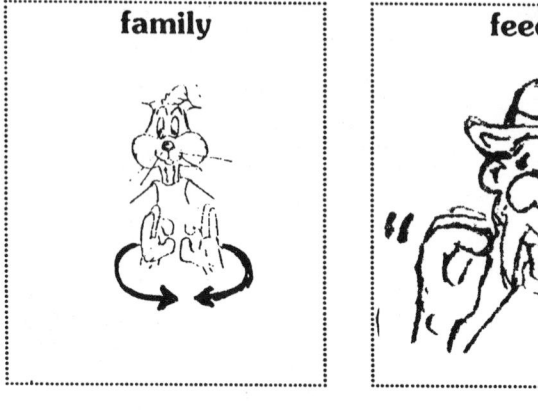

red

birds

in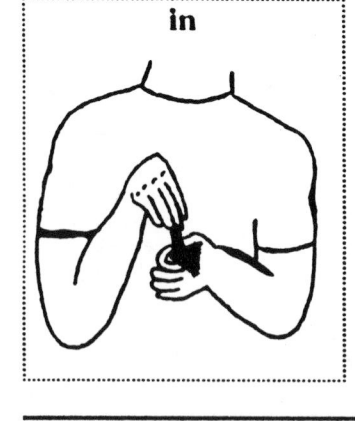

winter.

Painting by Bruce Miller

The following bird-feeding suggestions are from *Mother Nature's Michigan* by Oscar (Ozzie) Warbach, Michigan Department of Natural Resources. 1990, 96 pp.

FEEDING BIRDS IN WINTER

SONG SPARROW
TREE SPARROW
*DOWNY WOODPECKER
*NUTHATCH
*TUFTED TITMOUSE
CARDINAL
BLUEJAY
JUNCO
*CHICKADEE

* - SUET EATERS

A GOOD PLACE FOR FEEDERS IS NEAR SHRUBBERY (EVERGREENS ARE BEST). THIS FURNISHES WIND PROTECTION AND A SENSE OF SECURITY.

HOWEVER —

FEEDERS CAN BE PLACED NEAR WINDOWS SO ENTIRE FAMILY CAN ENJOY THEM

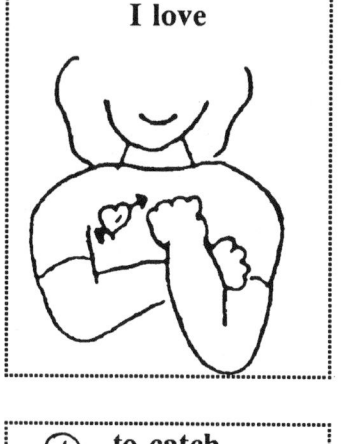

I love

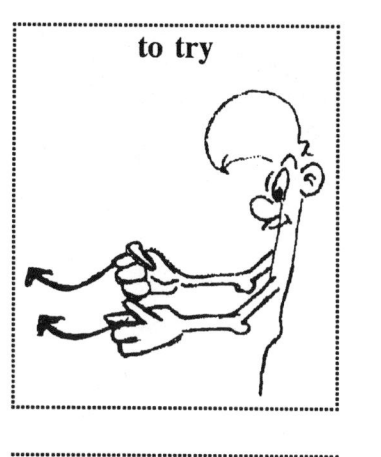

to try

to catch

turtles.

Photographs by Carl Sams II

<u>TURTLE TAG</u>:   The game is played the same as regular tag, except that when players are tagged, they must get down on all fours. To free the "turtle," an untagged player must crawl under the "turtle." For a fast game, name more than one player "IT," and have all the "IT"s trying to tag turtles.

--This game is reprinted with permission from *Aerobics With Fun* by Dr. Charles and Beth Kuntzleman and Michael and Gail McGlynn, Arbor Press, Spring Arbor, Michigan, 1984. It is part of the "Feelin' Good" program.

Mother

watches

brother,

sister

practice

walking.

Photograph by Jean Stolck

Baby rabbit 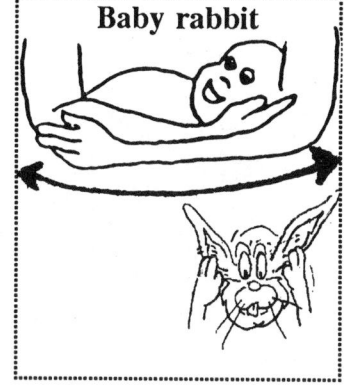	**is hiding.** 
No. 	**The rabbit, it** 
was 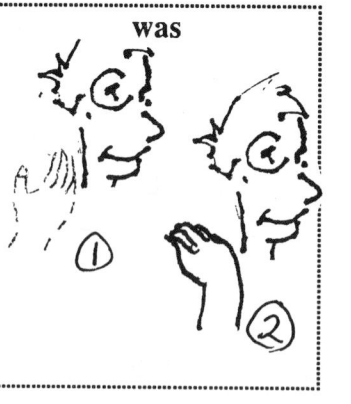	**found.** 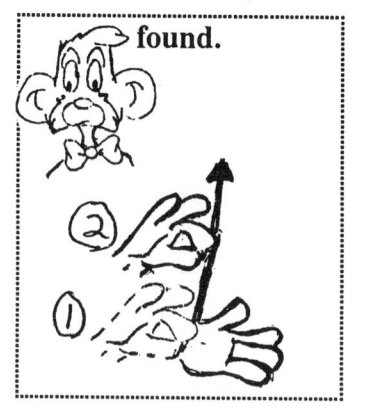

Painting by Tammy Laye

Yes,

I know

the man;

he

makes

muffins, cookies.

1991 Back-to-Back Exchange classes (France and Michigan) visited the Jiffy Mix company. They met "the muffin man." (French boys, photograph by Terry Robbins)

Find wordsigns for your favorite songs (like "Do You Know the Muffin Man?"). It's easy to remember the wordsigns when you already know the song. School choirs surprise parents with "He's Got the Whole World in His Hands" in French, German, Spanish, and Sign languages.

le français
Madame Stahl

1. **le babouin** = baboon
2. **le blaireau** = badger
3. **la chauve-souris** = bat
4. **l'ours** (m), **l'ourse** (f) = bear
5. **le castor** = beaver
6. **le boeuf** = beef (steer)
7. **l'oiseau** (m) = bird
8. **le taureau** = bull
9. **le lapereau** = bunny
10. **le veau** = calf
11. **le chameau** = camel
12. **le chat, la chatte** = cat
13. **la chenille** = caterpillar
14. **le poulet, le poussin** = chicken
15. **le chimpanzé** = chimpanzee
16. **le cacatoës** = cockatoo ('tiel?)
17. **le puma** = puma, cougar
18. **la vache** = cow
19. **le cancre** = crab
20. **le crabe** = crab
21. **le daim** = fallow deer
22. **le cerf** = red deer
23. **le chien, la chienne** = dog
24. **l'âne** (m) = donkey
25. **le canard** = duck
26. **l'aigle** (m) = eagle
27. **l'éléphant** (m), **l'éléphante** (f) = elephant
28. **le poisson** = fish
29. **le renard** = fox
30. **la grenouille** = frog
31. **la girafe** = giraffe

32. **la chèvre** = goat
33. **le chevreau** = young goat, kid
34. **le poisson rouge** = goldfish
35. **l'oie** (f) = goose
36. **le gorille** = gorilla
37. **la marmotte d'Amérique** = groundhog
38. **le cobaye** = guinea pig
39. **le hamster** = hamster
40. **le lièvre** = hare
41. **la poule** = hen
42. **l'hippopotame** (m,f) = hippo
43. **le cheval** = horse
44. **le kangourou** = kangaroo
45. **le chevreau** = young goat, kid
46. **le chaton** = kitten
47. **l'agneau** (m) = lamb
48. **le léopard** = leopard
49. **le lion, la lionne** = lion
50. **le lézard** = lizard
51. **le homard** = lobster
52. **le singe** = monkey
53. **la souris** = mouse
54. **la pieuvre** = octopus
55. **l'opossum** (m) = opossum
56. **l'orang-outan** (m) = orangutan
57. **la loutre** = otter
58. **le hibou** = owl
59. **la panthère** = panther
60. **la perruche** = parakeet
61. **le perroquet** = parrot

62. **le pingouin** = penguin
63. **le cochon** = pig
64. **le porceau** = pig
65. **le porc-épic** = porcupine
66. **la sarigue de Virginie** = possum
67. **le puma** = puma, cougar
68. **le lapin** = rabbit
69. **le raton laveur** = raccoon
70. **le rat** = rat
71. **le serpent à sonnettes** = rattlesnake
72. **la renne** = reindeer
73. **le rhinocéros** = rhino
74. **le coq** = rooster
75. **le phoque** = seal
76. **l'otarie** (f) = sea-lion
77. **le mouton** = sheep
78. **la crevette** = shrimp
79. **la mouffette** = skunk
80. **le calmar** = squid
81. **l'écureuil** (m) = squirrel
82. **le cygne** = swan
83. **le tigre, la tigresse** = tiger
84. **le crapaud** = toad
85. **la dinde, le dindon** = turkey(f,m)
86. **le morse** = walrus
87. **la baleine** = whale
88. **le loup, la louve** = wolf
89. **le louveteau** = wolfcub
90. **la marmotte** = woodchuck
91. **le zèbre** = zébra

Welcome to 2nd Grade

WELCOME TO 2ND GRADE!

Story and sketches by Girl Scout Brownie
Troop 579 (Allen Elementary School), Huron
Valley Council of Girl Scouts, Ann Arbor,
Michigan

**Kelly Bredernitz, Nicole Chisolm,
Erin Clark, Meredith Davis,
Samantha Emerick, Jennifer Fry,
Elizabeth Garcia, Melissa Gibney,
Elizabeth Hall, Anna Helvie,
Joanna Hetrick, Erin Keeler,
Janiston Kersey, Teiara Massey,
Ryan Maxwell, Sarah Meyer,
Chimo Mogbo, Heather Myers, and
Sarah Shiek (Troop Leader:
Debbie Hetrick)**

Photographs, Graphics, Layout: Marilyn Meyer
In the Woods used with permission

Adapted to sign language by Barbara Robbins,
ROBBINSPING PUBLICATIONS, a nonprofit,
educational organization.

Welcome to 2nd Grade

Welcome to

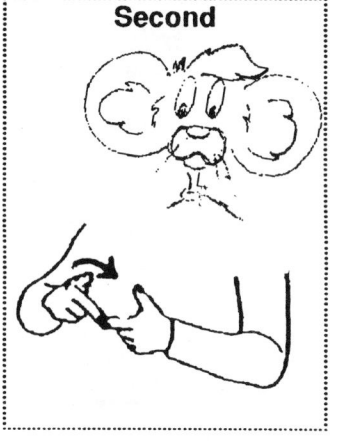

Second

Grade!

Hello!

We are

girls

seven

and

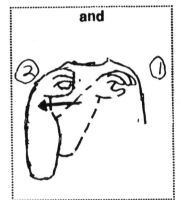

eight

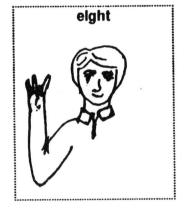

years

old.

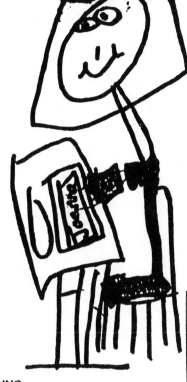

Joanna

FINGER SPELLING

Not *every* word has a wordsign. Words that don't have wordsigns, like a person's name, can be spelled using a finger alphabet. This alphabet is shown in the box to the right.

Can you figure out the message below?

ANSWER: Hello

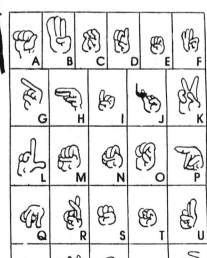

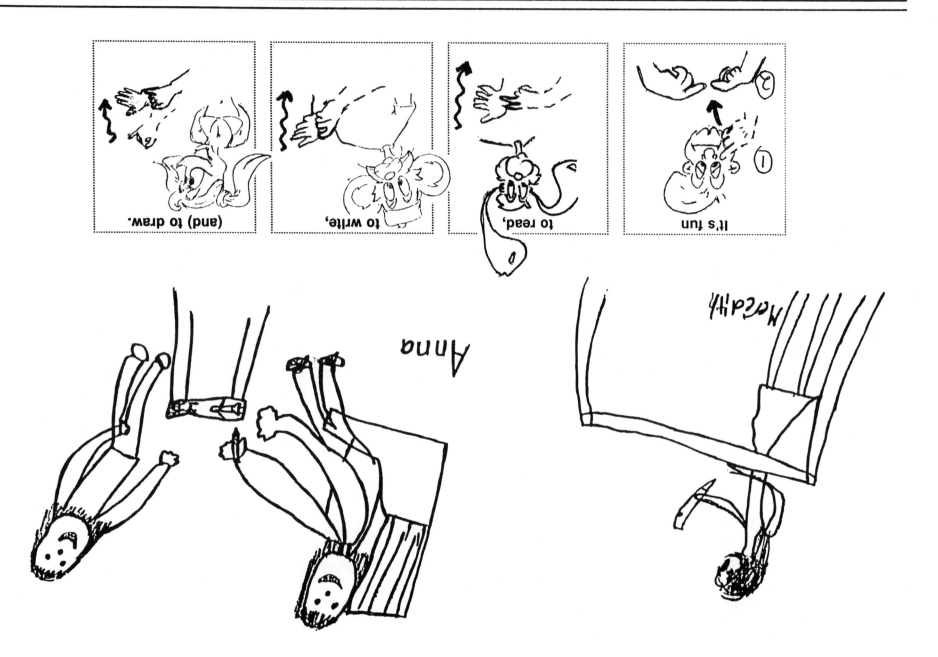

(and) to draw.

to write,

to read,

It's fun

Anna

Meredith

to sing,

and

to talk.

We	laugh	about
		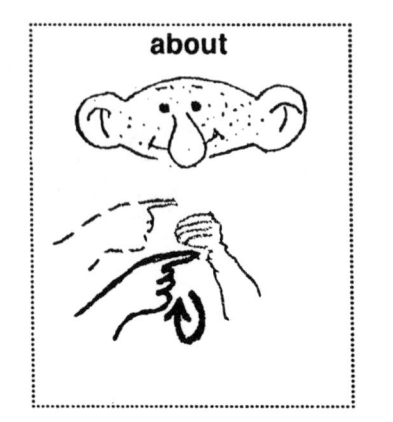

silly	boys
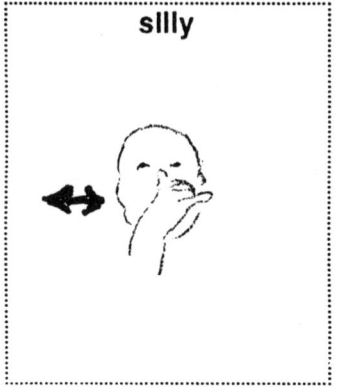	

In our	class.

Heather

When

school

is finished,

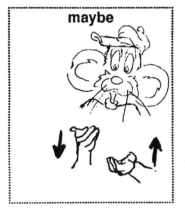

maybe

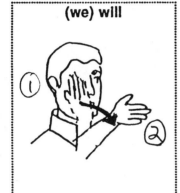

(we) will

jump rope

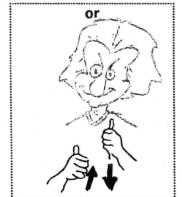

or

skate.

FAMILY-FUN IDEAS

<u>Crossword Puzzles</u>: Substitute signs for the letters needed to complete crossword puzzles. Take turns giving answers.

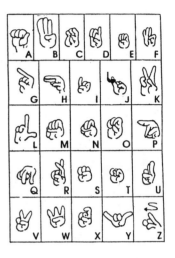

<u>Count the Ways</u>: Have a contest to see how many "signs" people use every day! Winner is the person who demonstrates the most signs.

<u>Other Storybooks, Games, and Videotapes</u>: Gallaudet University Bookstore has many materials available about sign language and hearing disabilities.

Gallaudet University Bookstore
Gallaudet
Kendall Green
PO Box 300
Washington, DC 20002
1-800-672-6720

Melissa

I

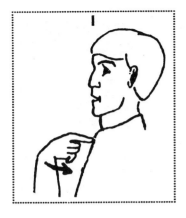

like

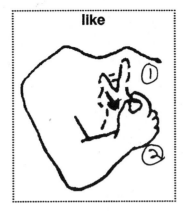

to play

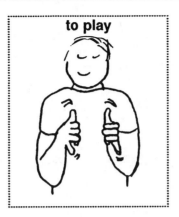

together with

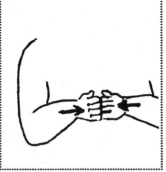

friends.

(On) Saturday

Mom,

Dad

help

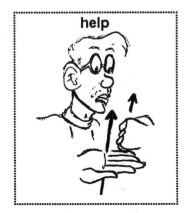

us

go

camping.

In the Woods

I went for a walk in the woods one day.

I hoped to find animal friends and play.

A rabbit, a squirrel, or a chipmunk would do.

But I couldn't find anyone. Could you?

So, I sat down on an old tree trunk.

And to my surprise I was joined by a skunk.

I looked at him, and he looked at me.

Then both of us were buzzed by a bee.

To the left, next to a great big rock,

Lo and behold! There sat a fox.

I smiled and grinned from ear to ear.

It was nice in the woods - with my friends sitting near.

It's a cold

day.
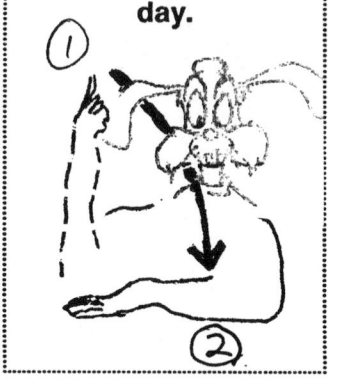

Make
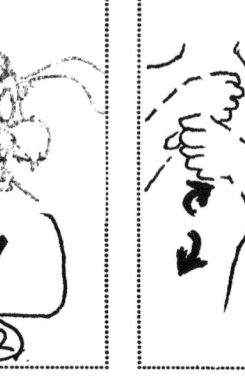

a fire.

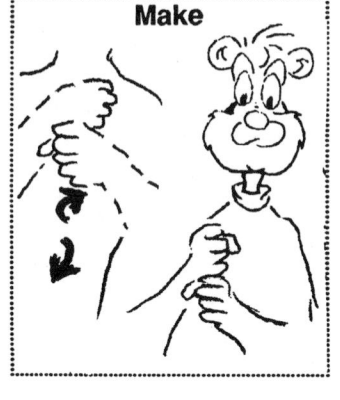
(I love you)

Cook
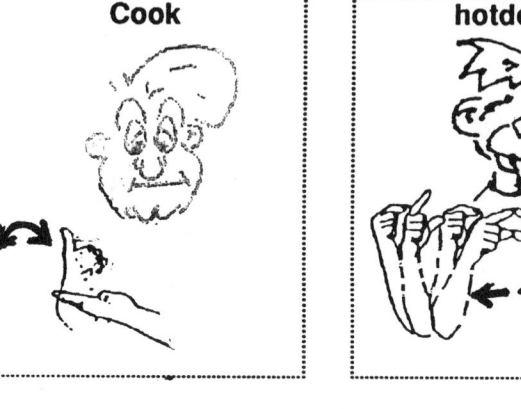

hotdogs.
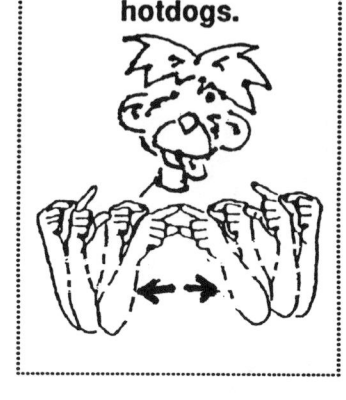

CHILDREN'S SONG

Five little hotdogs frying in the pan.
The grease got hot and one went BAM! (Clap hands)
Four little hotdogs frying in the pan.
The grease got hot and one went BAM! (Clap)
Three little...Two little...
One little hot dog frying in the pan.
The grease got hot and one went Bam! (Clap)
No little hotdogs frying in the pan.
The grease got hot and the pan went BAM!
(Clap LOUD)

Author Unknown

Sarah M.

We

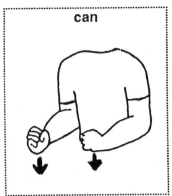
can

make

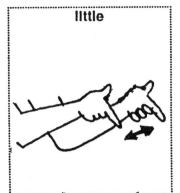
little

wooden

boats

to go

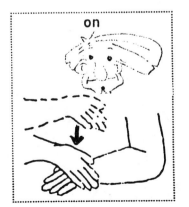
on

the lake.

Drink

hot

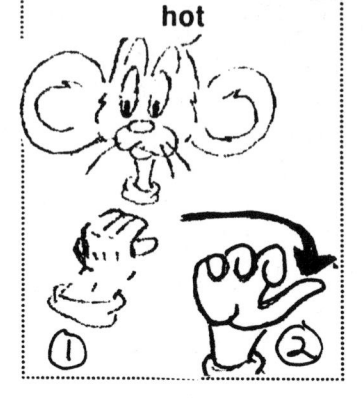

chocolate

and

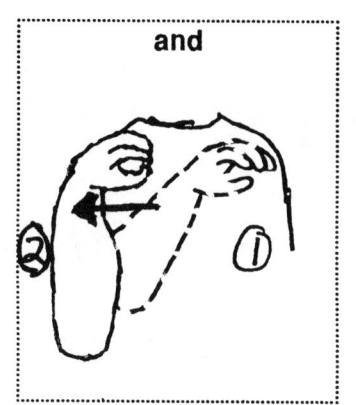

eat

marshmallows.

Chimo

THIS IS FUN!

Even people who can hear perfectly use sign language every day. You're using sign language when you wave at someone across a football stadium, when you point and put your finger to your lips in the library, and when you surprise someone. Do you use a "secret code" to talk silently?

Welcome to 2nd Grade

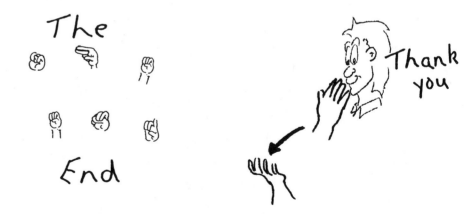

The

End

Thank you

Quiet, peaceful.

A good friend.

ASK YOUR LIBRARY for more sign language information. Teacher guides are also available from the National Grange Deaf Activities, Michigan United Conservation Clubs TRACKS® Magazine, and Robbinspring Publications.

One week we visited six classes in three school districts. The teachers invited us for different reasons, as follows:

1. Enhance Grade 2 health text 2-page deafness unit. Three Deaf mothers discussed how our minimal hearing ability affects our lives and how we handle it. Included demonstrations with Hearing-Ear dog, telecommunication device for the Deaf, and Sign Language storytelling. **RESULT:** Answered kids' questions from the point of view of personal experiences.

2. Supplement Grade 5 communication unit that does not mention Signing. Taught wordsigns in preparation for a Silent Day. **RESULT:** Children performed Pledge of Allegiance in Sign Language for returning Desert Storm soldiers.

3. Help Grade 3 with goal to befriend neighboring class of Deaf kids. **RESULT:** They play together at gym and recess now.

4. Get Deaf kids' ideas for more signbooks. **RESULT:** They helped provide constructive suggestions for our programs.

5. Grade 5, going to France with French class now visiting from there. **RESULT:** French student added French so this book uses the four main languages of our nation.

6. Allow a shy Hearing child of Deaf parents to use our teddybear puppet and Sign stories for Grade 3 classmates. **RESULT:** Students also used puppet to try some Signing. School Concert included songs in Sign for eight Deaf parents in the audience.

Letter to the Editor, TRACKS® magazine

I Like tracks Because of the sign language. Crane is the easiest to do so far. We learned how to do crane and keep our water clean. Keep our water clean is easier to do the short way spelling would take A lot longer. This is the short way........

Sincerly,
Justin

1 time

TRACKS® magazine is published by Michigan United Conservation Clubs. Since February 1990, its Teacher's Guide has included a sign language section, contributed by Robbinspring Publications. Editor Christie Bleck reports that the teachers asked her to continue this feature.

Life in the Woods

5

Painting by Marian Anderson

Story written by Marian Anderson
Adapted into sign language by Barbara Robbins

Life	in	the woods
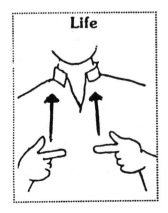	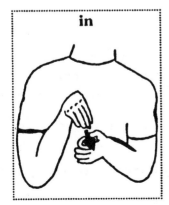	

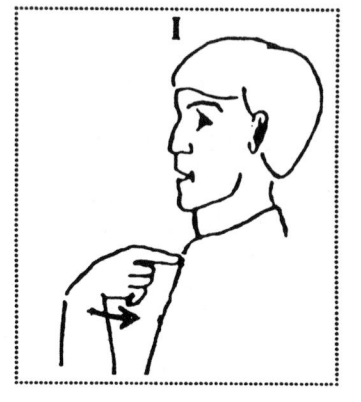

I

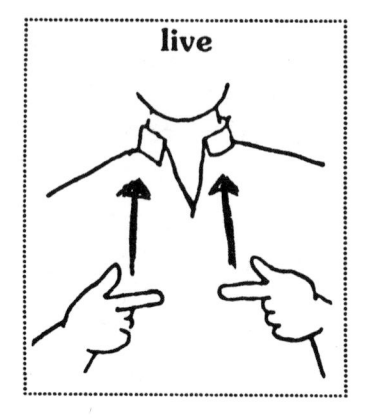

live

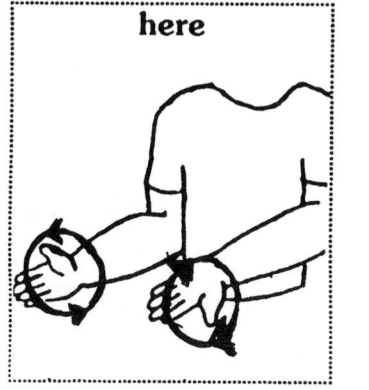

here

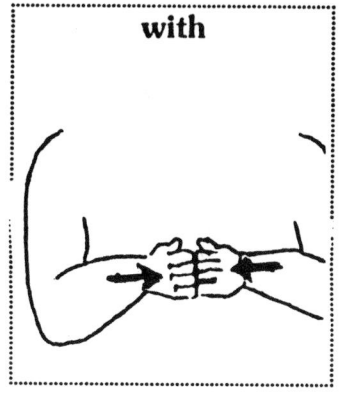

with

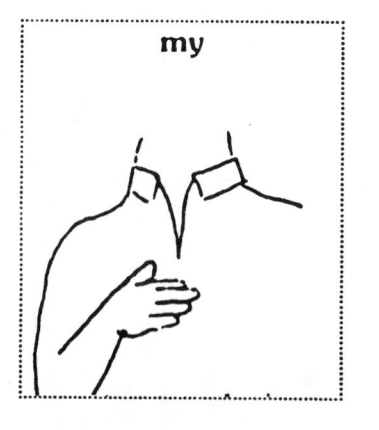

my

family

Photograph of Supervisor C.T. (True) Huntwork and helper at lumber camp, Curtis, MI, 1920

My	new	house	was made of
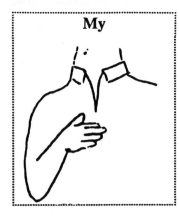	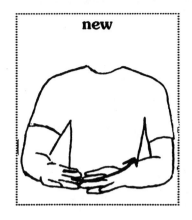		

big	trees	we	chopped.
	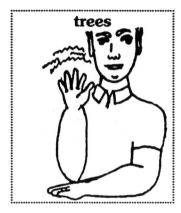		

Dad	finished	building	our	home.
		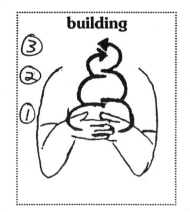		

We

are near

a beautiful

lake.

Trees

protect
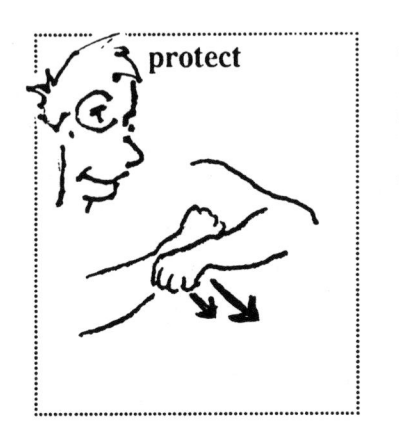

us.

The flowers

are pretty

in
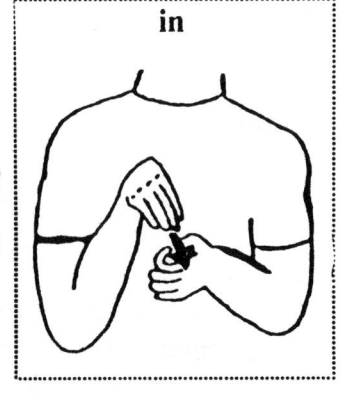

the spring.

Mother

has

a garden

where

the sun

shines

through

the trees.

We	**finished**	**building**	**a fence.**
		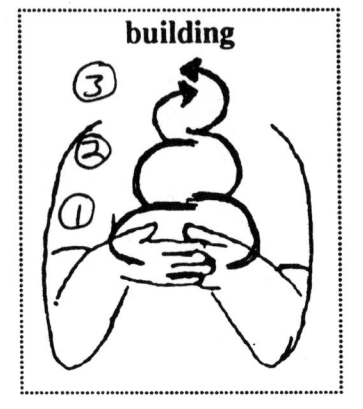	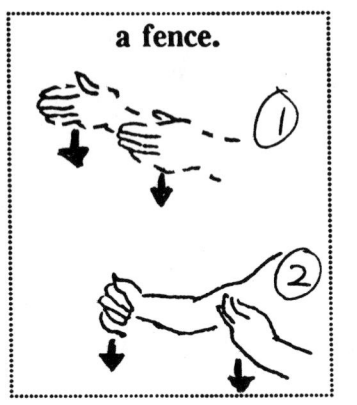

Now	**deer**	**and**	**rabbits**
		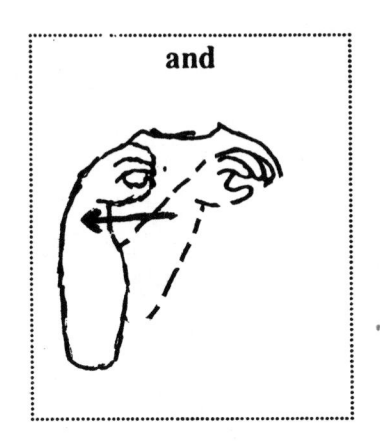	

can't	**eat**	**our**	**plants.**

We have many friends.

They are animals and birds.

The birds sing songs.

Painting by Marian Anderson

When | it becomes | winter,

I | help | make | Christmas | wreaths

with | some parts | picked | from | trees.

Squirrels

visited

yesterday.

Again

tomorrow?

I don't know.

Sketches by Michael Glenn Monroe

It's wonderful	to see	the deer	play.
	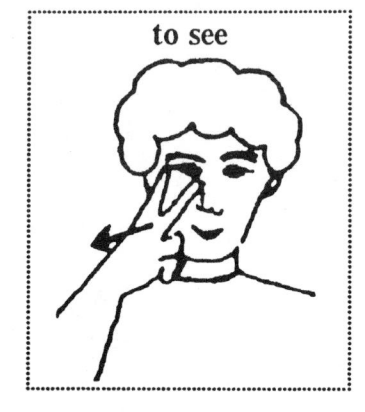		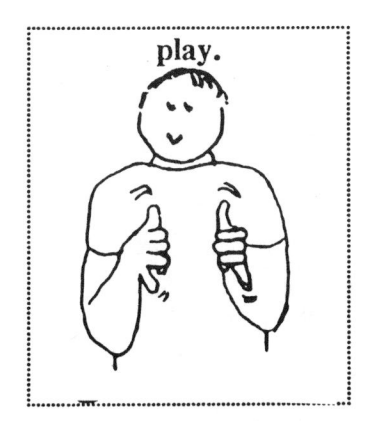

Maybe	butterflies	bring
		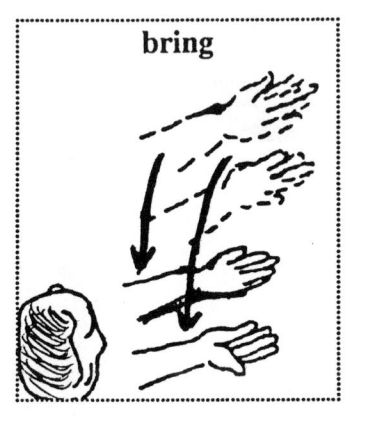

messages from	heaven.
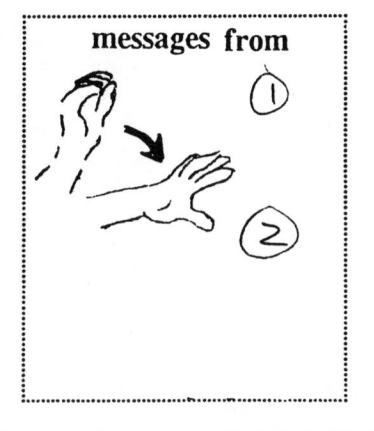	

She smiles for me again
As she walks in the breeze
With two little girls —
Listening to them,
Admiring, encouraging, enjoying them—
In the flowering fields
           — as always

         bhr

Sketch by R. L. Poisson, text by Barbara Robbins

Butterflies by Susan Falcone

Forest

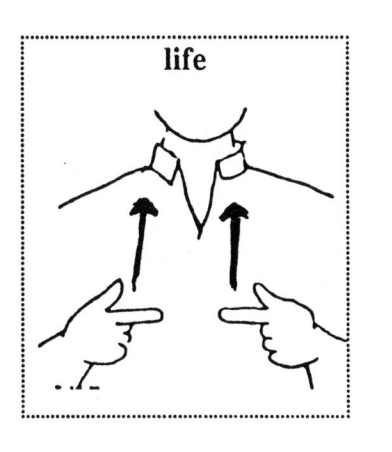

life

needs

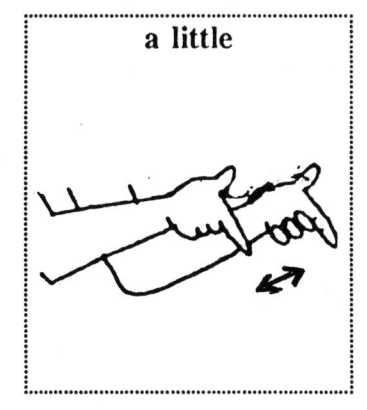

a little

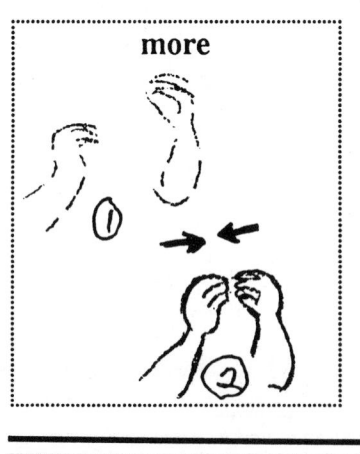

more

work,

Robbinspring Publications

Dear Barbara,

We so enjoyed your presentation at our spring camp last year that we sincerely hope you will do it again. We will have a new group of students who will be able to learn a lot from you. We'd like to use the same format as last year, unless you feel something else might work better. Do you still have the same booklets? Any new ones? Your shirts were a big hit also; I hope they'll be available again as well.

Sincerely yours,

Rikki Gans
Webster Elementary School
Livonia, Michigan

but

the effort

is fun

and

worth it.

Painting by Marian Anderson

We enjoyed your visit with us. We used more sign language from your books. The children learn quickly. When I asked them what they remembered from when you were here, they responded with:

A, B, C	(Jeffery R.)
baby	(Philip)
boy	(Lindsay)
clapping	(Tony)
grandfather	(Jeffrey B.)
grandmother	(Joel)
hamburger	(Dustin)
milk	(Tonya)
mother	(Kayla)
pancake	(Sam)
pop	(Nicole)
tree	(Sarah)
turtle	(Brian)
welcome	(Richelle)

Thank you for taking the time to come into our room. Your work is very well accepted by children.

Gratefully,

Joan Hibbard, Teacher
Developmental Kindergarten
Iron River, Michigan

Practice in front of a mirror!

Painting by James Killen

Dogs: **They** **go to** **school**

to learn **to help** **blind** **or**

deaf **or** **other** **people.**

I	**have**	**a TDD**	**typing**	**telephone.**
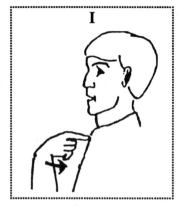	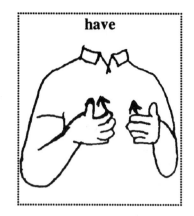	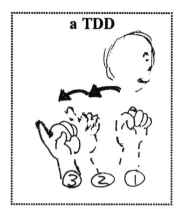	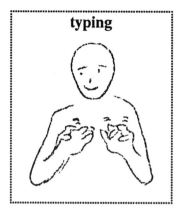	

I call	**to buy**	**pizza!**	**Pizza!**

P	**I**	**ZZ**	**A!**
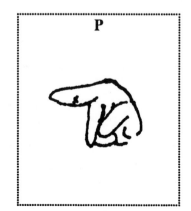	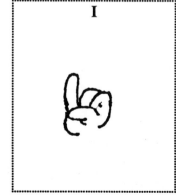		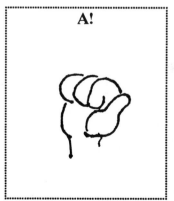

The sign for pizza and other words may vary in different towns. I think this is like speakers' accents.

I take my TDD on trips, to call the airline, car repair, church, hospital, hotel, pizza and other stores. Our 3-yr-old used the airport payphone for me when I could not hear. Now some payphones have TDDs.

Michigan has a TDD relay service. I use it to call someone who does not have a TDD (for example, the doctor). A relay person talks to the person I call, then types to me.

Hearing-impaired people now have telephone access to Michigan's major state parks, thanks to volunteer members of the Telephone Pioneers of Michigan. "Now, the hearing-impaired have, for the first time, telephone access to state parks information and camping reservations," Department of Natural Resources Director Roland Harmes said. "And, just as important, campers with hearing-impaired relatives at home have this equipment available."

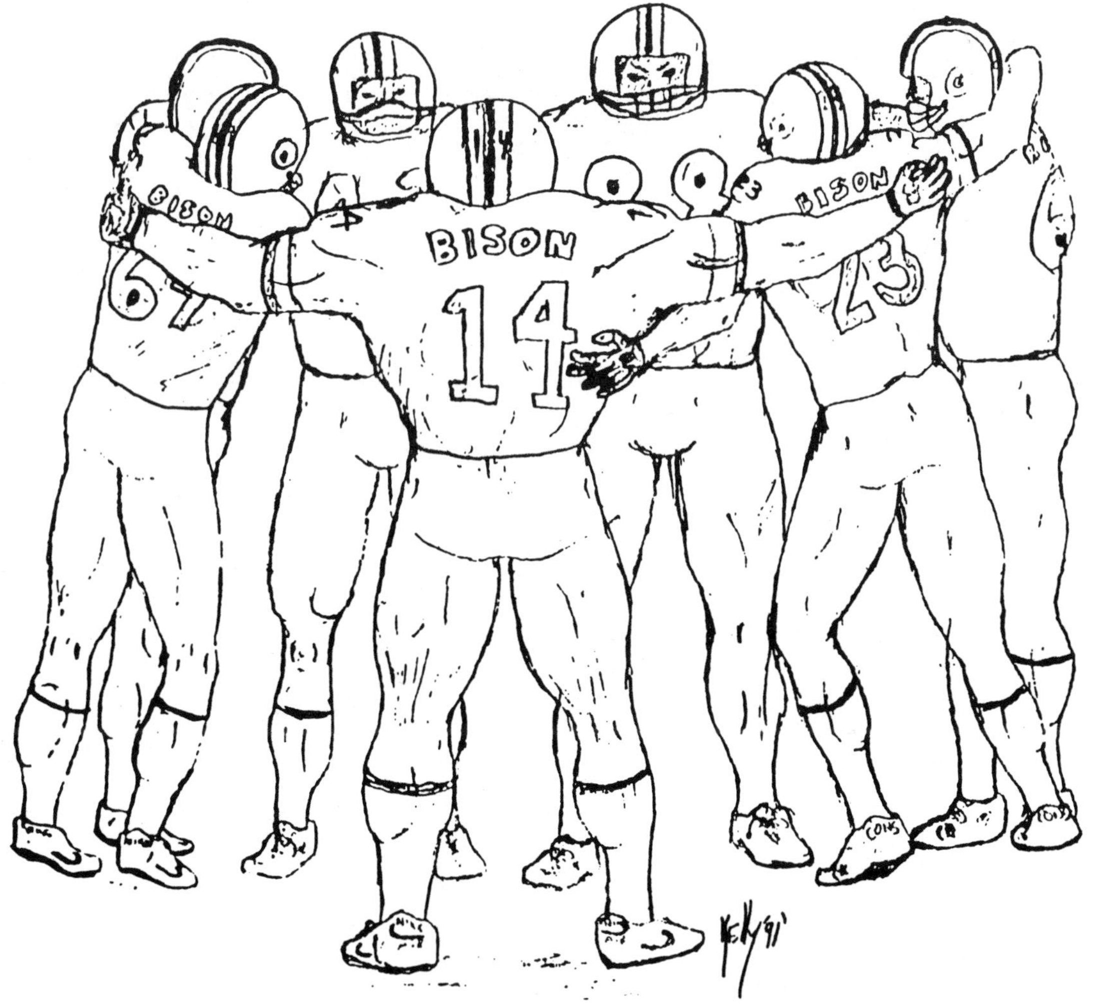

Gallaudet University

Sketch by Joshua Kelly depicts Gallaudet team intent on reading their quarterback's hidden hand signals

I bet the deaf faculty and students order pizza with TDDs.

Who	started	hiding

sign	language?	A team,
	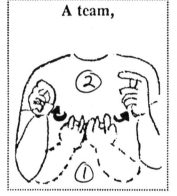	

deaf	football	players.	Why?
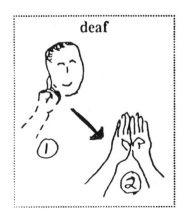		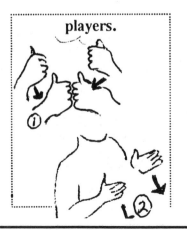	

What other sports use a form of sign language?

Does your coach ever change the sign language your team uses?

Why do referees use sign language?

What signs do umpires use?

Can they hear?

Hmmmmm, that's a good question.

Think about it!

Answer:

Gallaudet University players invented the football huddle.

I wonder how long ago.

It was such a good idea everyone uses it now.

NATIONAL HUNTING AND FISHING DAY,

near you, every fall:

For two consecutive years **HANK WILLIAMS, JR.,** the popular singer, was Honorary Chairman of National Hunting & Fishing Day. Do you know some of the songs he recorded?

He believes YOU deserve the right to enjoy all aspects of the out–of–doors. Hank has met more than his share of hurdles life throws in front of "what some call the common man."

A man,

Hank Williams, Jr.

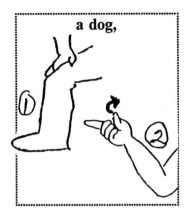

a dog,

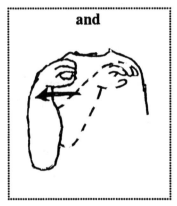

and

a song.

On a hunting trip "in 1975, he slid 500 feet down
a mountain in the Rockies, landing head first
on a boulder....Waiting...in the snow,...
Hank had a powerful revelation––he wanted
desperately to live, and, amazingly, he did."

He used the winning spirit that all people
display when working to overcome serious injury
and when facing the challenge of being
handicapped, temporarily or permanently.

"With a sense of wonder," Hank frequently returns
to the out-of-doors. "Then I feel the cool peace
of the mountain touch me....and I realize, once again,
that sometimes it takes the mountains to give
a man perspective, to show him that there are
things bigger than his exalted heights."

––from <u>Living Proof</u>, his autobiography

HELP ENCOURAGE Equal Access Recreation during
National Hunting and Fishing Day activities near you.

My

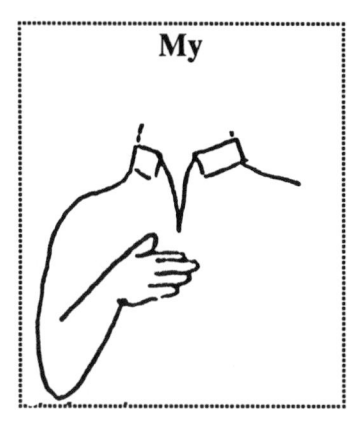

husband

helps

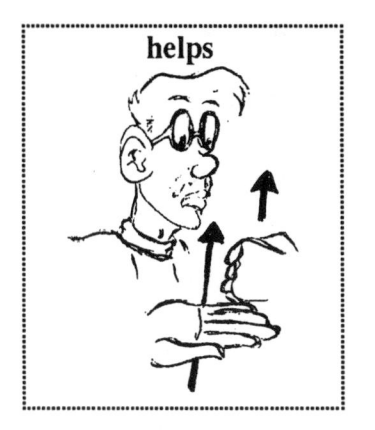

Barbara Robbins at OUTDOORS FOREVER® Handicap–Awareness Fishing Day. "I could not hear the captain telling me how to land the fish. I did it wrong, but caught the fish."
(Photo by Barb and Dan's son, Scott.)

me

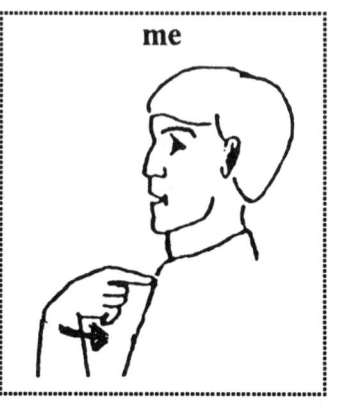

catch

very

Children Involved with Deaf People:

Our fourth child taught us how kids naturally adapt to situations. He taught himself to touch people before speaking to them; that's how he got **ME** to listen.

He also used his toy telephone upside down. I wore my hearing aid in a shirt pocket and had to tip the phone to "listen" in my pocket. He copied my way.

big

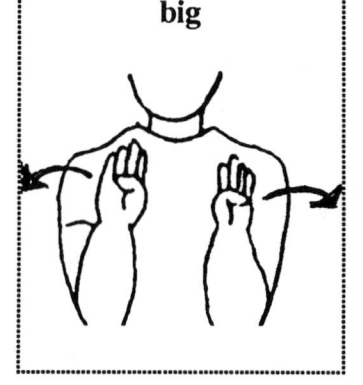

fish.

Hooray!

In high school he earned a Ham Radio license with a friend, Mike, who has many skills. For instance, Mike repaired the carburetor on Scott's car. At a computer swap meet the boys went to, Mike bought a talking computer program. Later, we learned Mike is blind. From infancy, Scott knew about handicaps, so he sees a person's skills before any limitations.

Five

families

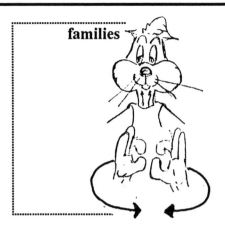

glad

to know

two

languages.

Matt is BUSY with his parents. Among other things, his dad, Tim, is Cub Scout Packmaster. His mom, Sandy, leads a Girl Scout Brownie troop of deaf girls and works at a school. Tim caught a bigger fish than Barb's (above) at OUTDOORS FOREVER® Handicap–Awareness Day in Oscoda, MI.

Historically, in Martha's Vineyard island communities, sign language was used. Read about it in Everyone Here Spoke Sign Language, by N. Groce.

Why do you suppose that happened?

Do you know people in a community near the water?
Do you go fishing with them?
Did you ever catch a fish? How big was it?
How big a pan did the cook need to use for your fish?
Did you use your hands to answer these questions?

PUZZLE: How do divers talk underwater?

Sarah, Emily, and Rachel
(photo by their parents)

Carrie and Darryl
(photo by their parents)

Sarah practiced the sign language she was introduced to in her Girl Scout Brownie troop. She shared her skill with her sisters, Emily and Rachel.

Their parents shared this story with us:

"Because our oldest daughter brought your sign language story booklets home from a meeting, our whole family enjoyed this new activity."

"We are proud to report, also, that our 3-year-old learned even more, because she was able to become friends with a hearing-impaired classmate at nursery school. The teacher says they 'chat' constantly."

Carrie's First-Place bowling trophy stands with other family awards. She started with a team at age 5, Darryl started at age 3. Darryl is in Little League and they are both Scouts. Darryl earns Tiger Cubscout pawprints. Carrie and Darryl used sign language before they could talk.

Their dad, Doug, graduated from the Technical Vocational Institute (St. Paul, MN). He has worked for the same printing company since 1978. He is also a skilled carpenter. The family attends church where an interpreter signs for deaf people.

Their mom, Amy, helps sick people and also trains dogs. Their own dog alerts them to sounds they do not hear. When it was their turn to host Darryl's den meeting, Doug and Amy asked an ambulance crew to come with sirens, flashing lights, and emergency equipment. The boys were fascinated.

Each family pictured on these four pages uses sign language for a different reason. Think about it.

Katie was 2½ when doctors learned she is hearing-impaired.

Katie is lucky. Her mom helped organize a preschool so children like her don't wait until kindergarten to learn a language. Every preschooler wants to talk with their brothers, sisters, parents, grandparents, and neighbors NOW. The teacher wears hearing aids, too.

Katie's family all use sign language. She is now a Girl Scout and helps her troop understand the many things she can do. She is glad when restaurant people know sign language because she likes to order her own meal and receive the right food, not something by mistake. Her brother, Joshua, drew sketches for this book.

EASY PRACTICE IDEAS:

YOU STARTED with a familiar song, like "Old MacDonald Had a Farm." You added action words for sentences with animal names.

DID YOU FIND word "families," groups that are similar, like *we, our, us? me, my? bird, duck? eat, feed? find, found?*

NOW PRACTICE. Sign-spell words that do not have their own wordsigns. The best way is to repeat common letter combinations like in a typing class: a–t, b–a–t, c–a–t, f–a–t, h–a–t, m–a–t, p–a–t, r–a–t, s–a–t, v–a–t. Then continue with: c–o–t, d–o–t, g–o–t, h–o–t, j–o–t, n–o–t, p–o–t, r–o–t, t–o–t, and so on.

MANY wordsigns paint a scene or picture an idea. That is, to say "slow," you dr–a–a–a–g one hand up the other arm. Have you noticed that wordsigns often perform an action while you hold your hand in the form of that word's first letter?

PERHAPS reading and math and history even became more fun as you started "thinking" in Sign Language. Try Signing a favorite story from your textbook, at your own reading level, and let us know what happened. Did it stir up enthusiasm or feel like an extra chore?

IN YOUR COMMUNITY, find more information at libraries. We find that deaf people are eager to have you try to "talk" with them. They will help you learn more phrases. Enjoy meeting them often.

WATCH OUT, adults. Kids learn these concepts FAST. I gave them the page from the Sign dictionary showing "can" (a fist–pounding sign of determination). They immediately taught me a lot about "caterpillars" from the same page. Caterpillars climb, tickle, eat, feel soft, etc.

bear

caterpillar

chicken

cow

elephant

frog

giraffe

insect, bug

lion

monkey

mosquito

owl

pig

tiger

wolf

This is fun.

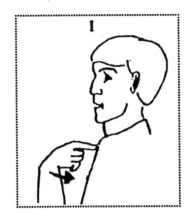

I

won't

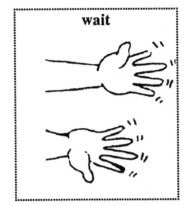

wait

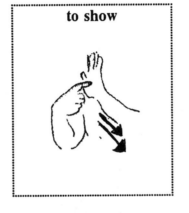

to show

Grandpa

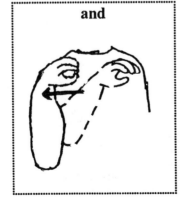

and

Grandma.

"How can I help?"

ALMOST HALF of the "hearing" children and teachers we meet know someone who has a hearing problem.

YOU CAN HELP someone "hear" you easily if you stand where light shines on your face. That way, they can "see" your words while you talk.

I can't hear in the dark. Can you?
I can't understand people talking behind me. Can you?

CHIDREN CREATE stories. We don't need to tell you that kids enjoy animal action stories. They tie animal names with other basic words in Sign and make corny jokes. In craft classes they produce their own booklets.

MUSIC TEACHERS find their choir eager for more signing. They surprise families with favorites like "He's Got the Whole World in His Hands" in several languages. "Silent Night" is especially beautiful performed in sign language.

COSTUMES created by two dozen youngsters (age 4–12) was summer fun. They performed a play in sign for the library's reading program.

ENJOY this quiet (if you're lucky) activity. And **please include grandparents in the fun.**

Handicapped

children

often say:

(Photograph by Ronald G. Robbins)

"Hi!" Jenny has no handicap, especially when trying out a new language she can have fun using with anyone.

(Photo by Barb Sebring)

"Most of all,

I want

a friend."

Nothing means more to deaf children than a friend who can speak their own language. Using sign language, this 2½-foot Honey Bear® is just what the teacher, parent, and therapist need for a creative new way to teach and entertain children. Honey sits on your lap, and your hands become Honey's hands. She keeps their attention; she reassures them; she tells them stories. Watch the children come alive with excitement at this huggable, lovable new little friend. Washable, nonallergenic, and safe.

by Quiet Bears™
PO Box 6542
Ventura CA 93006
(805) 647-0609

Honey,

the Quiet Bear®

says:

"I 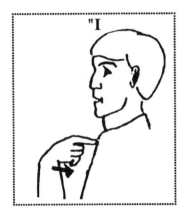	will 	teach 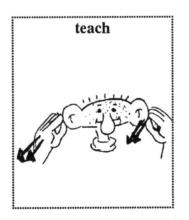
Hearing 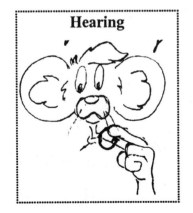	children 	to sign." 

Jeremy learned to help Honey tell a story in sign language, when author Barb Robbins visited his school.

(Photo by Barb Sebring)

"Then,

you

can

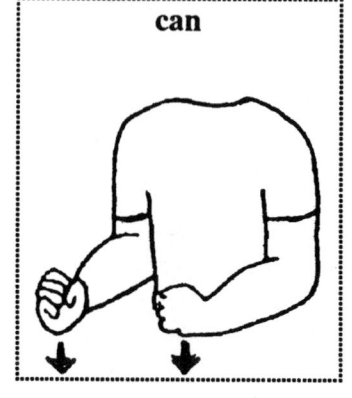

have

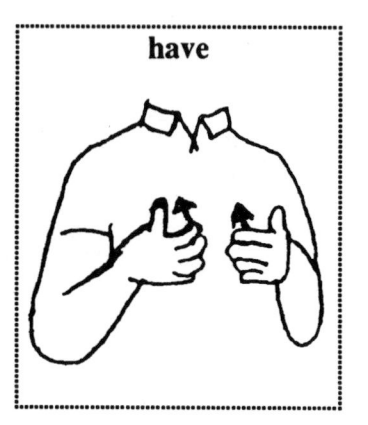

fun

with

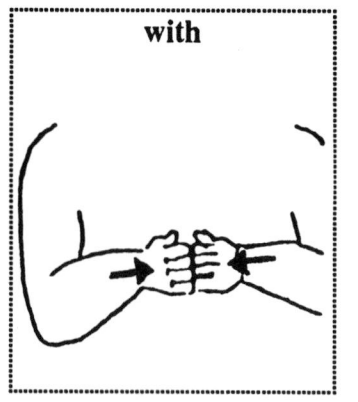

a friend."

the Signing Teddy Bear

"I love you."

Honey has become friends with many children around the world. She even helps them talk about problems they may have, such as shyness, illness, a handicap, or a brother who teases too much. Would you like Honey to live at your church or school library? Parent groups often order one.

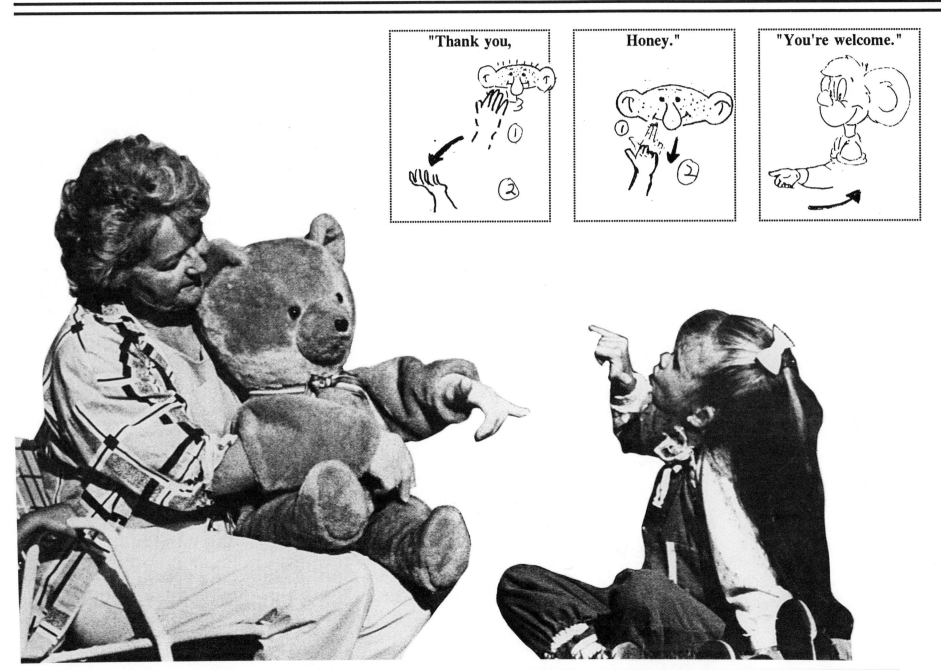

I feel sick.

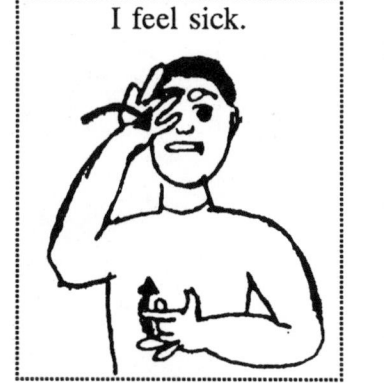

My throat hurts.

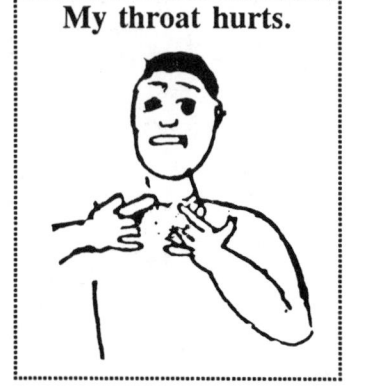

I can't

talk.

The nurse

signs:

We	can	help
	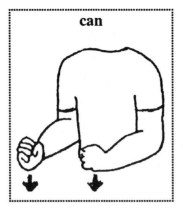	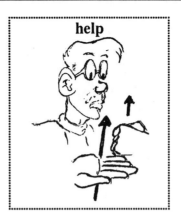
your	body	become
	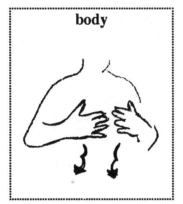	
strong	again.	
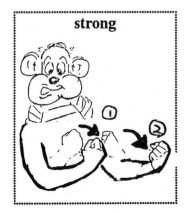	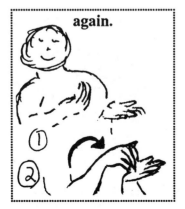	

"Will I get deaf?"

Children at schools often ask me if they will get deaf. I don't know. I am sure there are many causes of hearing loss. Ask your doctor's advice, especially if you are worried and have trouble hearing sometimes. He or she will help you learn how to help your body stay well.

I was 45 when I learned how to help my hearing a little. Maybe I didn't ask enough doctors earlier for help with increasing deafness. I just bought hearing aids. The doctors who figured out possible causes and ways to help with my hearing problem follow the philosophies presented in the Suggested Resource List on Page 103.

I know now that some of MY problem is related to allergies that I have had since I was a baby. My family and I did not recognize the connection, because I learned to talk and to play the violin. I did wonder how my third-grade teacher heard the kids answer her from the back of the room, though. If you think you may have a hearing problem, feel free to ask several doctors about the trouble you are experiencing.

About 15 of every 100 people have hearing loss and must learn to accept and deal with it. That means, in each classroom of 30 students, five will probably have some hearing loss. And several will discuss ear tubes.

I quit a job because I could not accept the difficulty I began having when I answered the office telephone. We need not be afraid. We can still enjoy life many ways. I wish I could hear spring peepers and geese in the spring, but I can still remember those good sounds.

brings

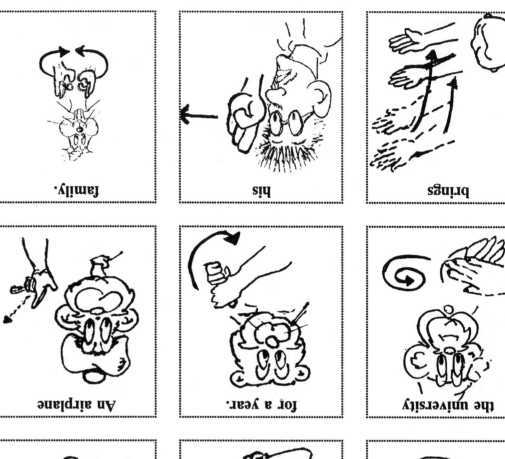

his

family.

the university

for a year.

An airplane

A doctor,

he

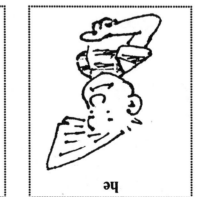

visits

DOMINO'S PIZZA

Scouts

teach

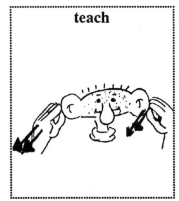

the son,

daughter

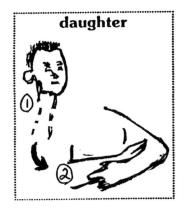

a new

language.

The family

returns

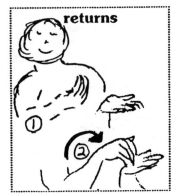

home.

One of the Girl Scout Brownies who helped write Chapter 4 of this book was a visiting student from Europe. Her father had been invited by the university to participate in some medical research. When the work was completed, the family went back overseas, but with many new friends here in the United States.

*Children with no disability perform her sign language play, **Fitness Witness**, using several handicapper tools of independence. Author Barbara Robbins is in the background while Paige Conat, Reading Specialist at the Jackson (Michigan) District Library offers encouragement (above). A participant's family watches (below).*
(Photographs by the Jackson Citizen Patriot newspaper)

People

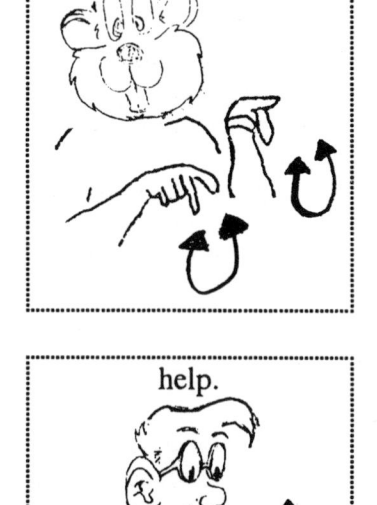

need

help.

Now

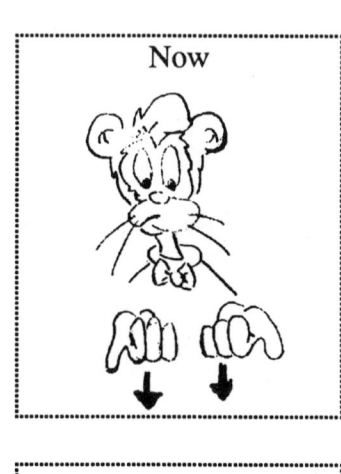

you

can

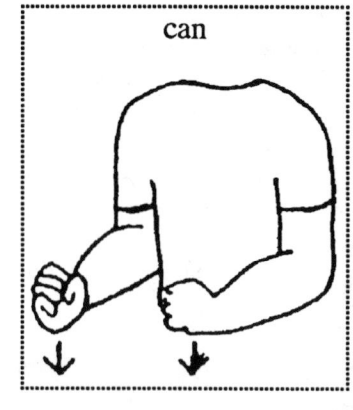

help.

Thank you!

The only woman to go to the North Pole is a Special Education teacher.

To learn how she survived falling into the Arctic Ocean, see our suggested reading on Page 5.

Sketch by Gayle Swinford

Acknowledgments and Credits

Foremost, my husband Dan supports this project, though it took thousands of family hours and dollars. His "Now what?" challenges me to take a fledgling idea and figure out how to fly with it. He encourages me to develop Robbinspring Publications as an independent business. Even though I became deaf after we were married in 1953, we're still a team - his ultimate compliment to me.

Children and their families deserve credit for showing me the best paths to follow. They tried their hand at sign language with concepts that developed into this book collection. I was welcomed in Ann Arbor, Davison, Farmington Hills, Flint, Hillsdale, Horton, Iron River, 20 Jackson organizations, Jonesville, Lansing, Livonia, Parma, Plymouth, Southfield, Spring Arbor, Stambaugh, Webberville, and Williamston. Teachers, librarians, and community leaders cared about my project goals and chose to offer the opportunity to their students again and again, especially Barb and Bob Badertscher, Christie Bleck, Paige Conat, Maggie Couling, Savitra Damodaran, Daryl Devine, Jerry Eicholt, Howard Henry, Debbie Hettrick, Gordon Holton, Juanita Ray, and Jean Ykimoff.

How do they use signing? In 1980, parents Flo Baerren and Anita Fischer led a dozen children (aged 3 to 12) to produce a sign language play at the library. Our students also teach others, without telling me: The May 15, 1991 *Jackson Citizen Patriot* featured 5th graders who performed the Pledge of Allegiance in sign language at a program recognizing soldiers returning from Desert Storm. Denise Cavins and others at the newspaper continue to present inspiring photostories of our activities.

Wildlife artists Al Agnew, Marian Anderson, Gary Bortolotti, Tim Callahan, Rod Crossman, Susan Falcone, Lane Kendrick, Jim Killen, Tammy Laye, Catherine McClung, Bruce Miller, Mike Monroe, Carl Sams II, Jean Stoick, Nick vanFrankenhuysen, and Jerry Yarnell generously share their work and concepts.

"Tough love" came from attorney Art Benedetto, √ CheckMARK computer consultants Mark and Marilyn Meyer, commercial artist Cindy Lyons, publishing advisors Kate Bandos and Jerry Jenkins, and deaf culture leader Lenore Coscarelli.

Financial supporters: Chelsea Milling (Jiffy Mix), John Christian, Civitan Clubs of Jackson and of Plymouth-Canton, Consumers Power Foundation, Jackson Community Foundation, Jackson Society for Handicapped Children and Adults, Livonia Public Schools, Malloy Lithographing, North Jackson Lions, and Parke-Davis Pharmaceutical Research Division of Warner-Lambert Company offer us a future.

Suggested Resource List

Catalogs: 1) Gallaudet University Bookstore, 800 Florida Ave. NE, Washington DC 20002, at the only university designed specifically for the deaf, carries a wide variety of enlightening titles, including signed videocassettes which teach at your own pace and sources to "learn by computer." 2) TJ Publishers, 817 Silver Springs Ave. #206, Silver Springs MD 20910-4617 presents timely, valid Sign Language & deaf culture material.

Deaf Culture: *A Hug Just Isn't Enough* (Ferris), *Another Handful of Stories* (Rosen, Kannapel), *Children of a Lesser God* (Medoff), *Dancing Without Music* (Benderly), *Everyone Here Spoke Sign Language* (Groce), *Great Deaf Americans* (Panara), *Other Side of Silence* (Neissen), *Outsiders in a Hearing World* (Higgins), *Seeing Voices* (Sacks), all helped me become less scared and more accepting of hearing loss.

Dictionaries: *American Sign Language Concise Dictionary* (Sternberg), *The American Sign Language Phrase Book* (Fant), *Joy of Signing* (Riekehof), *Signing Exact English* (Gustason, Pfetzing, Zawolkow), *Signing--How to Speak With Your Hands* (Costello), and *Signs for Me* (Bahan and Dannis). *Signs Across the Country* (Gallaudet) shows "accents" that flavor the language. Look for the sections in these titles which also teach, in terms you and I can understand, the pictorial, conceptual grammar of American Sign Language.

Favorite Songs: *Lift Up Your Hands* I and II (Gadling, Pekorny, Riekohof) and *Music in Motion* (Modern Signs Press).

"Hearing" Health: ASK SEVERAL PHYSICIANS. *Brain Allergies* (Philpott), *Impossible Child* and *Is This Your Child?* (both by Rapp), *It's Not Your Fault You're Fat* (Mandell), *Tracking Down Hidden Food Allergy* (Crook), *Yeast Syndrome* (Trowbridge), all written by physicians, include information that applies to at least part of my hearing problem. I discovered my hearing ability CHANGES. By learning specifically what creates these changes in me, I now have some control over the situation although I will always wear hearing aids. I do not intimate these books cure anyone.

Signed Stories: *Chris Gets Ear Tubes* (Pace), *Hand Talk* (Mary Beth), *I Have a Sister, My Sister is Deaf* (Peterson), *I Was So Mad* (Modern Signs Press), *Sesame Street Sign Language Fun* (Bove), *Tracks®* magazine (Michigan United Conservation Clubs Teachers' Guide), and *Young Man* (Robbins, in press) to accompany *Christ Commission* (Mandino, Bantam Books).

Annotated Index of Wordsigns

(NOTE: Use more motion for verbs than for nouns.)

Index of Instructor Notes

Index of Activities